Enthusiastic Tracking
The Step-By-Step Training Handbook
Second Edition

William (Sil) Sanders

Rime Publications
Stanwood
1998

Rime Publications
33101 44th Ave NW, Stanwood WA 98292
Sil@Starband.net
360-629-6434 (voice), 360-629-3537 (fax)

Artwork in phase 2, 3, and 6 is used with the kind permission of artist Mario Salacone.

Pictures used with the kind permission of the dog's owners:
- The cover dog is Ch. Rime's Quonquering Hero UDX TDX MX AXJ JE,
- The dog with the author is Ch. Rime's Game Goddess TDX,
- The Belgian Tervuren is Ch. Pine Mist's Lone Ranger UDT.

The author appreciates the many people who critically commented on the first edition including, in particular, Grace Blair. He also expresses his special gratitude to the proofreaders of the second edition: Jean Dieden and Anne Sanders, as well as the heroic last minute efforts of Jill Jones, editor extraordinaire, who corrected numerous additional typos.

Library of Congress Catalog Card Number: 98-96127

Sanders, William R.
    Enthusiastic tracking : the step-by-step training handbook / William R. (Sil) Sanders. – 2nd ed.
        160 p. 28 cm.
    Includes bibliographical references and index.
    LC Call No.: SF428.75.S26 1998
    Dewey No.: 636.7/0886 21
    ISBN 1-892119-22-6
    1. Tracking dog training.   I. Title.   II. Title: Dog Training
                                           98-96127

Fifth Printing, 2005.

Printed in the United States of America.

To Alicia for her patience with a novice trainer

and

to Mr. Q for his expressiveness about how scent changes along the track.

Alicia was Ch. Rime's Alicia Aquena CDX TDX CG who became the first Westie to earn a TDX.

Mr. Q is Ch. Rime's Quonquering Hero UDX TDX MX AXJ JE, the second Westie to earn a TDX.

Contents

Introduction

Tracking is a fun activity for a dog and handler to enjoy together. The general idea is for the dog to follow the scent left by a person walking through an area and to find an article dropped by that person. It turns out dogs are quite good at this and naturally enjoy using their noses. We do not teach the dog how to use their noses; they are naturally thousands of times better at using their noses than we are at using our noses. We are going to teach the dog to stay with a track until he finds the article. We teach this by showing him that it is always lots of fun to do so!

The major premise behind the Enthusiastic Tracking training technique can be summarized by listing the three most important issues in successful dog tracking: motivation, motivation, and motivation. This analogy to the old real estate joke reminds us that no matter how well-trained our dog is, he will only follow a scent (which we cannot smell ourselves), lead us down the track (which we cannot see ourselves), solve the scenting problems along the way (which we can at best only partially understand), and find the article at the end if he is strongly motivated to do so.

Tracking is unique in dog sport in that the dog knows what to do and the handler must read his dog and follow him. Although we carefully structure our initial training tracks so the handler does know exactly where the track is located, when the dog is tested, the dog must be prepared to assume the leadership role.

In addition to the supreme importance of motivation, the dog must master numerous scenting and problem solving skills before he will be successful. This training method provides ample opportunity for the dog to master these skills.

Tracking is a team sport in the truest sense of the concept. Although the dog is the master of scent and the team leader, the handler has a critical support role to play for the team to be successful. The first important aspect of this support role is for the handler to trust and believe his or her dog when the dog is committed to a track. The second aspect is when a scenting problem causes a dog to lose the track, the handler must organize the dog's search and encourage him to search nearby quadrants or areas that he has not yet covered.

This training method first develops basic scenting skills in the dog while building motivation to stay committed to the track. Then the method develops handler skills in reading the dog and organizing searches for lost tracks. Finally, the method refines the basic skills of the dog and handler until they are fully prepared to handle any situation they are likely to face in a test.

This book first describes training for the AKC Tracking Dog title and then it goes on to cover TDX training. The training is also suitable for CKC's tracking program since both the Canadian titles are tested with tracks that are similar to but a little bit simpler than their AKC counterparts. AKC's variable surface tracking program is new and this method has not yet served as the basis for training dogs on to the VST title. So, no recommendation is made in that regard.

If you and your dog are well prepared, you and your dog will pass the TD test and you will have an excellent chance of passing the TDX test. You only get to pass once since most tracking tests are full. So, enjoy your training! It will account for 99% of your tracking experience. Make every training session fun for you and your dog. Focus on that fun and success in the goal of passing the tests will follow.

In this introduction, I discuss an overview of scent and how a dog works scent. The remaining chapters deal with a specific schedule of training activities that is designed to mold you and your dog into a confident tracking team.

Scent

Since the strength of scent found on most tracks is too faint for human detection, we have to observe how a dog reacts to scent to learn how scent is affected by various conditions. We can never directly know the experience of scenting a two-hour old track. However, by careful observation of many dogs tracking, we can learn much about scent and about a dog's detection of scent.

When a person walks through a field, he or she leaves five different types of scent. By understanding these types of scent, we can understand how to better train our dogs to track.

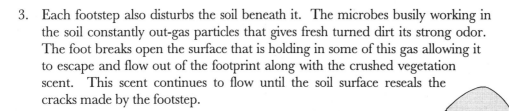

1. A person is constantly giving off particles or rafts from their skin, their hair and their breath. If your nose is sensitive enough, these particles smell like the person. They float through the air and leave scent over a wide area to each side of the walker's path. Wind and air turbulence distributes the scent in a very complex way. Typical scenting behavior indicates that there is a distinct change in scent about ten to fifteen feet to each side of the walker's path.

2. As a person walks through a vegetated area, each foot crushes and bruises the grass or weeds underneath it. The damaged stalks and leaves give off odor particles much like a mowed lawn gives off odor. I imagine each footprint as a miniature mowed lawn that is as obvious to the dog's sensitive nose as a big mowed lawn is to my nose. This strong flow of crushed vegetation scent flows up out of the footprint and floats downwind. The odor particles are influenced by similar wind and air turbulence that effect the personal scent. These footprints keep emitting scent until the plant damage heals, so crushed vegetation scent appears to last quite a long time.

3. Each footstep also disturbs the soil beneath it. The microbes busily working in the soil constantly out-gas particles that gives fresh turned dirt its strong odor. The foot breaks open the surface that is holding in some of this gas allowing it to escape and flow out of the footprint along with the crushed vegetation scent. This scent continues to flow until the soil surface reseals the cracks made by the footstep.

4. Each footstep also rubs off some particles of the shoe sole. This scent must smell exactly like the walker's shoe soles. Although apparently weaker than the first three types of scent, it does seem to be present and dogs can learn to follow it if the other normally stronger scents are unavailable.

5. In tracking, the walker leaves one or more articles along the track. The article scent comes from the material itself and from the personal odor particles transferred to the article while the tracklayer carried it. Many materials, such as leather, have quite strong intrinsic odors. In addition, many articles appear to absorb the tracklayer's personal scent quite effectively and therefore smell both like themselves and like their owner. The scent from most articles is quite strong and is spread out by the wind and air-currents over a wide area.

All five types of scent are available to the dog when following the track. The first four are available throughout the length of the track, while the fifth is available near the articles. The scent from these sources drifts in air currents, perhaps pooling in surface irregularities such as holes or clumps of vegetation, or near large objects such as trees or bushes.

In addition, the dog must distinguish the track scent from other competing scents that are also present in the field. For example, the scent of the undisturbed dirt, the scent of various weeds and other vegetation, and the track scent left by the numerous small animals that use the field must be distinguished from the main track scent.

Tracking has its jargon and a few special words are worth knowing. The scent cone is the area of strong scent close to the track. It often extends ten to fifteen feet or more to each side of the track. The distinct drop-off or change in scent at the edge of this scent cone is called the fringe.

There is much more that can be discussed about how scent moves in the wind, how scent is effected by age, humidity, and other environmental factors, and how the dog perceives it. The above five-part model is an adequate basis for starting your dog tracking. As your dog's training progresses, you can learn a great deal about scent by observing your dog's behavior.

Styles of Scent Work

There are numerous ways that dogs use their nose. Although this book focuses on tracking human scent, the dog's ability to do this work is related to its ability to do other scent work. It can be helpful to keep these other scenting work styles in mind when observing and understand a dog on a track.

Air scenting is a scenting style that is often used by dogs in search and rescue. Highly trained search and rescue dogs can detect the scent of a victim over long distances under the right wind conditions. These dogs can also switch into tracking mode when a track is available. These dogs and handlers choose the method to find and reach the victim the most quickly or the most reliably as conditions dictate. Although air scent is a valuable skill, it is not encouraged in the AKC and CKC tracking tests that are the focus of this book. Bloodhounds do have a trailing test where the dogs are encouraged to follow the air scent near a trail.

Tracking prey was an obvious evolutionary selection pressure that caused the dog to develop his excellent scenting ability. Many of today's suburban dogs show excellent natural scenting skill when given the opportunity to track prey. Since small animals may cross tracks in AKC and CKC tracking tests, we train the dog to stay on the original track and to ignore animal tracks. However, tracking dogs also excel in hunt tests and hunting trials when given the opportunity to do so.

Discrimination of articles touched by different people is a skill that is used in obedience as well as police work. Dogs can be trained to distinguish many different scents and to find articles discarded by a lost person in search and rescue as well as those discarded by fleeing suspects.

As your dog's tracking training progresses, it will be important to encourage the dog to follow the original track scent closely rather than allowing him to adopt broad ranging air scenting strategies or allowing him to follow animals that may have crossed his track. A dog that does try to adopt such strategies is making a very natural mistake. He should be gently guided toward the techniques that will allow him to develop into an expert tracker.

Training Philosophy

Motivation is the key factor in successful tracking, because a dog must lead us down the test track that is obvious to him no matter how invisible it is to us. Limp tracking line is a poor tool for pushing a dog twenty feet ahead of us, so we must develop and maintain a keen sense of joy in the dog when he is on the track. It is much easier to develop this relish for tracking on simple tracks that are known to the handler than to try to develop it on more difficult and complex tracks. Moreover, it is always better and more efficient to maintain this enthusiasm than it is to lose it and try to redevelop it later.

We build motivation and enthusiasm by rewarding the dog frequently in the beginning and withdrawing those rewards slowly and randomly. We maintain motivation by continuing all dogs on an intermittent schedule of random rewards.

Because motivation is the key factor in successful tracking, we avoid using any harsh corrections. Harsh corrections are likely to de-motivate the dog. We also structure the progression of the training so that at each step in the training, the dog is much more likely to succeed than fail. Failure is also likely to de-motivate the dog.

Although we avoid corrections, we will mold the dog's tracking behavior by gentle adjustments in line tension as well as by the use of food, play and praise rewards. This combination of reward and molding line tension encourages the dog to rapidly learn what is needed to find the rewards.

Whenever we have to help the dog, we adopt a very happy and positive attitude. We gladly show the dog what is the fun thing to do! A 40-acre tracking field is too small a place for frustration.

From the dog's point of view, staying right on the track should always be the easiest, the most fun and the most rewarding thing to do. It should still be fun to be near the track, just a little more work to get to the goodies. In those rare instances when the track get confusing, the handler happily shows the way to rewards. The dog should never know anything about failure or strong corrections on the tracking field.

Equipment

You will need a tracking harness. Get a non-restrictive harness -- one that does not have any straps across the sides of the shoulders. Silvia's Tack Box has a nice adjustable nylon harness (309) 797-9060. J & J also has nice nylon and leather harnesses (800) 642-2050. Several other vendors carry suitable harnesses as well.

Other basic equipment:

- articles such as an old leather glove and a cotton sock.

- forty-foot tracking line (1/8" mountaineering cord, 1/8" nylon parachute cord or 1" flat webbed cotton line for large strong dogs who like to pull).

- 8-12 tracking stakes. Old ski poles with their webs removed work well. Attach colorful surveyor's tape or flagging to each stake so it will be visible from a distance.

- container of water you can carry with you in a fanny pack.

- food such as hot dogs sliced into small pieces.

- a tracking journal.

Avoid using a thirty-foot tracking line. It is the most common length available in 1" flat webbing and so many people start out with the thirty-foot length. This big mistake will hurt your ability to handle difficult corners. So get that fifty-foot line and cut it down to length! If you track exclusively in Canada, you can use a fifty-foot line so you don't even have to cut it down to length.

Because I always train with food rewards, my schedule shows the food drops on the track maps. I can only recommend this approach for tracking teams that use food rewards. If you have a dog that is not motivated by food, see Ganz & Boyd's book mentioned below.

There is a minor art in slicing hotdogs for food drops. A dog senses as much reward from a small piece of food as a large one. For medium and large dogs, slices of hotdog the shape and thickness of a nickel work very well. They are large enough to be easily found and not too large to fill the dog. For small and toy dogs and puppies of all breeds, slice the hotdog lengthwise in half or quarter before slicing crosswise into nickel thickness. You must make the drop small enough that the dog is still hungry and rewarded after finding lots of them on a track. Slicing the hotdog thinner than a nickel causes them to dry out and be less appealing. Freshly cut moist hotdog nickels, or half-nickels, or quarter-nickels are the magic treat that I recommend.

Operant conditioning research indicates that the ideal reward size is 1/40th the dog's daily food intake. So if you want to use that as a guide, you will have a lot of research behind your choice. I have found the sizes I recommend above fairly close to their recommendation and that they work well in the context of tracking.

The figure at the right shows some typical equipment for TD training: a flag, a leather glove, a harness and a tracking line.

Suitable Land

I prefer to introduce a dog to tracking on grassy meadowland that is little used by other people. Because such land is soft, it takes a footprint well. Because the cover is seldom mowed, the taller vegetation holds the scent well. Because there are few conflicting footprints, the dog is less likely to be confused about its new task. I avoid pastureland where livestock creates a complex of conflicting hoof-prints and lawns where many people's footprints form a hidden labyrinth of cross-tracks.

Finding such uncontaminated land may be difficult but it is worth the effort, since it is easier for the dog to understand his task and to stay motivated. A confident dog may be exposed to contaminated land during all phases of training, but it is preferable to start phase 1, 3 and 5 on uncontaminated land. It is also wise to return to such land if the dog losses motivation after a long period of working less ideal land.

Look for undeveloped regional parks and preserves; silage, hay or idle fields; or carefully rotated pasture-land. You need 15-20 acres for a typical tracking session. Always obtain landowner permission before using the land. Many landowners will be happy to have you use their land if they understand what you are doing, if your dog is always on lead, and if you help keep it clean by picking up trash. Others may prefer that you go elsewhere.

It is fair to acknowledge that many excellent tracking trainers do not control the pristine nature of their tracking land as carefully as I do. Some trainers purposefully start in heavily trafficked schoolyards so their dog learns from the very beginning to ignore conflicting tracks. Although this may work with many dogs, I am unwilling to take the risk that the dog will be confused and lose motivation when learning a new task with too many uncontrolled variables.

Commitment

Although it is generally best to have a clear goal in mind when starting a new venture, you may or may not know enough about tracking at this point to set a clear goal. Your goal may be as limited as learning about tracking to as specific as having your new puppy earn all available tracking titles. Whatever your goal, this book and your own hard work can help you reach that goal.

AKC offers three tracking tests leading to four titles: Tracking Dog (TD), Tracking Dog Excellent (TDX), Variable Surface Tracker (VST), and Champion Tracker (CT). A dog must first earn his TD and then may work towards the TDX, the VST or both. A dog with both a TDX and a VST becomes at CT. The CKC offers TD and TDX titles for passing tests that are similar to their AKC counterparts.

The TD is typically earned on a 45-minute-old track that is 470 yards long with four corners. There is a flag at the start and one at 30 yards so the handler knows the initial direction of the track. The Canadian version of the test is similar although it typically has two corners. Almost any dog and handler team that can walk through a meadow can learn to pass this test by following the instruction in this book.

The TDX is typically earned on a 3-hour-old track that is 900 yards long and has seven corners. The main track has been crossed by two people about 90 minutes after the track was laid. The track will contain at least two additional obstacles that will challenge the dog's scenting ability and the handler skill in reading his dog. It is a difficult test with a low passing rate. The Canadian version of this test is similar although it uses a single person to cross the track and it uses less challenging obstacles. The first part of this book focuses on building a firm foundation for tracking; the second uses that foundation to support advanced training toward a TDX.

The VST is typically earned on a 3-hour-old track through an urban or suburban setting such as a typically college campus setting. The track is on land that many other people typically traverse and will use non-vegetated surfaces like gravel, cement and blacktop for much of its length and it will pass near large buildings. It uses lawns rather than wild meadows for most of its vegetated surfaces. Like the TDX, it is a difficult test with a low pass rate.

It is fair to wonder how long it might take to train a dog to his first tracking degree. The time depends on your dog's natural love of using his nose and learning to do 'things' for you, your prior knowledge and skill in dog training, and the focus you bring to bear on achieving your goals. The time also depends on how quickly you to get into a test.

In spite of this variation, we can estimate the length of time based on the number of times per week you are able to track. So the chart below shows a range of months of training where the smaller number applies to the quick to learn dog-handler teams and the larger number applies to more typical dog-handler teams. I do want to emphasize that there is nothing inherently better about quick-to-learn teams than typical teams except they learn faster. Teams that are more typical can definitely learn as well and can end up performing as well or better than the quick-to-learn teams.

Sessions Per Week	Months for Quick-to-Learn Dog-Handler Teams	Months for Typical Dog-Handler Teams
7	2	4
5	3	5
3	5	8
2	7	12

Many trainers are successful if they train the first two or three phases as rapidly as possible and then settle back into a less frequent schedule. Although this works for many people and dogs, it is more important to adopt a schedule that fits you and your dog's energy level and ability to dedicate time to this fun activity. At various times, I have successfully trained dogs using different schedules. One dog was successfully trained 7 days a week for the first four phases of training where we dropped down to 3 days a week. Another was trained less than once a week. My own most comfortable training schedule is three times a week. Experiment a little and see what works for you and your dog.

Whatever your level of training and your long term goals, setting short term goals and keeping them will give you and your dog a sense of immediate success and add to your motivation to continue. Practicing with a friend allows you to keep one another going when you might not feel like going out on your own.

This is one sport that you can and should practice in all types of weather. Heavy rain does not wash away the scent and strong wind does not blow it away. Nevertheless, they do effect the scent conditions and you and your dog should be used to working in them. When it comes time to be tested, a gale force squall is not going to cancel the test, so be prepared. You will enjoy (or at least tell yourself you enjoy) being out in the fresh air amidst nature's wonders. I certainly have seen more rainbows while tracking than while sitting in an office, so dress for the weather and enjoy it.

Most of us do most of our training in temperate conditions and avoid very hot and very cold weather. However, people have trained dogs to track in the summer in the desert and the winter in the north country. If you do attempt to train in very hot or very cold conditions, contact someone in your area that already does it to learn the local tricks to make it successful.

Other Resources

The focus of this book is on a particular training method that I have found to produce excellent tracking dogs of many different breeds and personality types. I hope it is complete enough to stand on its own. However, much can be learned from the other treatments of tracking and scent work found in several excellent books. I encourage you to add to your knowledge by also reading these tracking books. Several additional books are listed in the bibliography for those who want an extended library of tracking knowledge.

I recommend Glen R. Johnson's ***Tracking Dog - Theory And Methods,*** Arner Publications, Inc., Canastota, NY, 1977. This is the bible of restricted tracking and his tracking schedule and many of his techniques served as the basis from which I evolved the method described in this book. Much has been learned about tracking since this book was published. In particular, the introduction of TDX in this country in the early eighties led many of us to discard his double and triple laid tracking techniques that lead to confusion about track direction. In addition, we learned that many more dogs and handlers could succeed by avoiding as stressful a training schedule as he advocated. I strongly recommend to all serious tracking students the first three general chapters as well as the chapter on problem solving.

Another excellent book is Sandy Ganz & Susan Boyd, ***Tracking from the Ground Up***, Show-Me Publications, St. Louis, Missouri, 1992. This book is full of useful information and techniques that everyone should have in their bag of training techniques. If you are put off trying to follow my very detailed description of how to do every step in the process of training your dog, you may well find their training method easier to follow.

A book which combines a scientific approach to scent with practical dog training techniques is Milo Pearsall and Hugo Verbruggen, M.D., ***Scent***, Alpine Publications, Loveland, Colorado, 1982. Anyone who wants to extend their knowledge of scent beyond the basics must be aware of the extensive knowledge presented in this book.

A different type of book is Roy Hunter's ***Fun Nosework for Dogs***, Howln Moon Press, Eliot, ME, 1994. This is chuck full of fun and educational scent games to play with your dog. Play them just for fun, or play them to teach your dog how to pay more attention to his nose.

You will need a rulebook for the tests you intend to enter. The American Kennel Club's ***Tracking Regulations*** covers their TD, TDX and VST tests and is available from them at 5580 Centerview Drive, Suite 200, Raleigh, NC 27606-3390 or on the internet at www.akc.org. Other registries in the USA, such as the American Mixed Breed Owners Association, follow AKC's rules. The rules for tests in Canada are available from the Canadian Kennel Club.

If you are new to tracking, find a local class to attend. A good knowledgeable instructor can make all the difference in noticing you and your dog's problems and suggesting corrections. Ideally, find an instructor who is willing to work with you as you follow this schedule. If no instructor is available to you, track in a small group every week. Your tracking friends can offer you observations that you might fail to see yourself and you can learn a lot by observing your friends and their dogs. If no one else in your area is interested in tracking, just go do it yourself. Spend a little extra time reflecting on your performance and your dog's performance. Keep a detailed journal and review it regularly.

I also have had the privilege of learning from several national figures in the sport. Glen Johnson provided my initial exposure to tracking. His seminar taught numerous valuable training techniques which are still applicable today and which have been carried forward into this book. More recently, John Barnard, AKC Executive Field Representative for Tracking, has provided the sport with an integrated understanding of scent from the perspective of the police dog trainer, the scent researcher, as well as the AKC tracking enthusiast. Their understanding of scent and the scenting ability of a dog as well as their ability to teach others about scent have been of immense importance to the sport of tracking.

As valuable as each and everyone else have been to my education, my best teachers have been my own dogs. Alicia suffered many training mistakes and kept patiently guiding me because she loved to track so much. Mr. Q, who is the best natural tracking Westie I ever expect to see, solidified the importance I place on enthusiastic tracking and, through his expressive behavior at scent transitions, taught me a great deal about scent. Dorie, Aura, and Belle's difficulty understanding corners taught me to separate the issues of corners from the issue of crosswind tracking. Both Dessa and QT gave me the opportunity to train dogs who wanted to please me as much as themselves, not a common attitude in Westies.

Comments Welcome

I would appreciate your comments on this book so I can improve it. Send your comments to me at 33101 44th Ave NW, Stanwood, WA 98292-7106; 360-629-6434; Sil@Starband.net. So that I know which version your comments apply to, please reference this version's date (September 17, 2005) in any correspondence.

Feel free to comment on any aspect of the manual. I am particularly interested to know:

- if you can read and understand the tracking diagrams easily,

- if the form of the presentation makes what should be done clear,

- if the descriptions are clear,

- if the method of customizing the phase 7 tracking plan made sense,

- if you were able to train your dog by following this manual.

If you have Internet e-mail, you can join the Tracking List or the Tiny Trackers List. I currently participate in both of these lists and you can expect to get answers to your questions from a variety of tracking people from around the country and the world.

To subscribe to the Tracking List, access
http://www.smartgroups.com/groups/tracking

To subscribe to the Tiny Trackers List (for people with dogs under 25 pounds), or for CKC, visit
http://www.yahoogroups.com.

Use a search engine to find web sites dedicated to tracking. There are quite a few good sites with lots of interesting information about tracking.

Phase 1. Introducing the Dog to Tracking.

Purpose:

- Introduce the dog to tracking.
- Teach the dog that when we give him the command to track, there is something to find and his nose helps him find it.
- Teach the dog that tracking is fun.
- Teach the handler how to use the line to communicate with his dog.

Strategy:

- Start out with very short tracks where the dog will be frequently rewarded and find the article quickly.
- Extend the length of the tracks and the distance between the rewards gradually.
- First four sessions have the tracks going into the wind so the dog smells the track ahead of him.
- Last five sessions have the tracks going downwind so he will bring his nose down onto the track.
- Gradually increase the lead length as the dog starts to stay right on the track.
- Keep the dog unstressed and happy.

Schedule:

Session	Number of Tracks	Wind Direction	Track 1 Length	Track 2 Length	Track 3 Length	Total Length	Lead Length
1.0	Practice						
1.1	3	into	10	15	20	45	6'
1.2	3	into	10	20	40	70	6'
1.3	3	into	15	30	60	105	6'
1.4	3	into	20	40	80	140	10'
1.5	3	with	30	60	120	210	10'
1.6	3	with	40	80	160	280	10'
1.7	3	with	60	120	240	420	15'
1.8	3	with	80	160	320	560	15'
1.9	Review						

Discussion:

Make sure you have all your equipment and that you and the tracklayer understand your roles. If the tracklayer is new to tracking, show him on a pretend track without a dog. If both of you are new to tracking, practice tracklaying and handling without the dog. There is much detail in the description of the first session of tracks. The detail is there to help you visualize the best way to teach your dog so you will avoid problems in the future. Take the time now to become thoroughly familiar with the procedure so you can feel confident about what you are doing when you are training your dog. You and the tracklayer should communicate to the dog your overwhelming enthusiasm for tracking in a convincing manner. That is hard to do when you are uncertain what you are supposed to do.

Should you want to teach your dog all by yourself, you can be both the tracklayer and the handler. In this first phase, you can crate your dog at the start while you lay the track. For people with breeds that require large crates that are hard to carry into the training field, using a crate may be difficult. Starting all tracks from the edge of the field by a parking spot may be possible. If you are comfortable staking your dog out in the field, then doing so for the short period you are laying these tracks may be appropriate. In any case, just be sure the dog can see the track as you lay it.

The handler should not try to control the dog as in obedience. The dog needs the freedom and self-confidence to find the track himself. In training, the handler restrains the dog when he is not on the track, but does not correct the dog for being off the track.

Lead handling is very important. When the dog is exactly on the track, keep a light firm tension on the line with your hand at belly level. As the dog moves to the side, raise your hand gradually until it is over your head and increase the tension on the line. The further off the track the dog is, the higher your hand and the greater the tension. When the dog gets six feet off the track, your hand should be over your head and you should not be moving. Wait until the dog swings back toward the track, lowering your arm and the tension as he approaches the track, and take a step forward as he comes to the track. You are making it easy for the dog to stay on the track and hard to stray from the track.

Keep your lead hand directly in front of you. Do not move your hand back and forth to steer the dog because the dog will learn to take steering directions from you and will not learn to be responsible for finding the track himself. You are raising and lowering your hand to make it harder or easier for your dog to track, not to steer him. If you have a very large dog that pulls strongly off the track, raise your hand to the side of your head and keep your arm close to your body. This way you can use your full weight against the dog going off the track without moving your hand very far from center.

The **wind direction** is important. Do your best to lay the tracks into the wind or downwind as directed in the schedule. Sometimes the wind can shift direction between when you start to lay the track and when you run it. If the wind shifts from being along the track to blowing across the track on one track in a session, go ahead and run the track. Keep the dog on a short lead and keep him on the track. Don't let it happen too often, because the dog can learn some bad habits by tracking in cross winds at this early stage. It is better to re-lay a track that has been messed up by the wind than to lay many tracks in the future to correct a bad habit.

Dogs will indicate an article in many ways. You want to teach the dog to indicate it in a way that is easy for you to see. People have their dog touch the article, pick up the article, retrieve the article, sit at the article, or down at the article. Any of these methods work well. For the first few sessions, accept any behavior by the dog that demonstrates that the dog even notices the article. Gradually raise your standards and mold a particular article indication of your choice.

It is easy for a new handler to be optimistic for his dog and become frustrated if the dog does not get the idea immediately. Such expectations and frustrations are out of place. Since the dog can easily sense your frustration, keep such emotions completely blocked by being happy the whole time you are on the tracking field. Most dogs will get the idea during the first phase, but it does not matter when during this phase that he gains this knowledge. Just keep to the schedule and he will pick it up along the way.

Puppies and Toy Breeds: Start puppies as early as you want. As young as seven weeks is OK for many puppies since the work is fun and there are no corrections. Don't expect a young puppy to stay focused on the task as well as an older puppy or an adult. Make sure the puppy is enjoying it. If not, do something else with the puppy until he is a little older and can better understand what you want.

For puppies, use the same schedule but scale all distances in half. So the first session would have tracks of 5 yards, 7 yards and 10 yards with hotdogs every 2-3 yards along the track. For a young puppy, skip sessions 1.7 and 1.8. If the distances still seem long for your young puppy, scale the distances to a third. What is import to do is to start short and progress to longer tracks, not to follow any arbitrary distance schedule.

Physically small breeds, low energy breeds and low energy handlers should adapt the schedule by scaling all distances in half. It is better for your dog to succeed at shorter distances than to complete a longer track that exhausts him.

Enthusiastic Tracking Field Maps

The description of each training session in the book includes a field map that shows the tracklayer exactly how to lay the track and reminds the handler about important training issues.

If you wish to keep this book clean and dry, you will want to purchase a set of 4x6 index cards that shows the map for each session. They are also a handy way to keep your tracking log.

See the last page of this book for more information about the cards and how to order them.

A Dog's First Track

Mom has been talking about tracking all week and at long last we're going to see what this is all about. After a long wait, Mom gets me out of the car and we walk out into a field along with a rather nice man who smells faintly of hot dogs. The man keeps talking to me like we are bosom buddies, but I'm really paying more attention to the fresh wet grass underfoot.

Before we have gone very far, the man stops and Mom starts putting that funny harness on me. She practiced putting it on me yesterday; and to hear her tell it, she's the World's Greatest Engineer for getting it buckled around me.

Now the man starts calling me in a cutesy kind of way and holds out his hand to my nose. Sniff, Sniff! There seems to be something good in his hand! Yes, a most delectable morsel of hot dog comes my way, because, he says, I am a good girl (which is, of course, ever so true). The man waves another morsel under my nose and plops it into a glove. I strain against the harness to get some, but Mom holds me back as the man adds two more morsels to the glove.

He waves the glove in front of my face while saying silly things like "Watch the glove!" Of course, I'm watching the glove, it's full of goodies! Instead of giving it to me, he turns around and walks away. "Hey Mister, did you forget to give it to me?", I wonder. Nevertheless, he keeps talking to me in a loud excited voice as he walks away. Pretty quick, he spins around, waves the glove over his head, yells to me to watch him, and then lays the glove to the ground. He turns again and quickly walks away from the spot, then circles back to Mom and me.

As soon as he is back, Mom downs me into his footstep and tells me to "Find it!". That should be simple enough; it's right out ahead here someplace. If I just scamper out there, I'll find it for sure. Off I go, but Mom keeps my harness on a short lead.

As I let her tug me to the side, I run into a hot dog on the ground. Wow, I never knew that hot dogs grew in the meadow — we should come here more often. Well, I'd better check for more hot dog plants nearby. Mom keeps saying "Find it!" and keeps me on a short lead. This keeps my scampers crossing the path that by the smell of it the glove-man made. Pretty soon, we come across another hot dog plant which is oh so yummy to find. This field of hot dogs must be the greatest natural wonder of the world, so we are off again to find some more.

We continue to cross the glove man's footprints as I search for more hot dog plants. Sniff sniff! — Sniff sniff! — I think the morsel laden glove must be nearby — Just over to the left — Oh yes, here it is — Yummy! Mom comes up and tells me what a Super Girl I am, and plays with me and the glove. I think this tracking is going to be fun, but I wonder why they don't call it hot-dogging.

Session 1.0

Purpose:
- Introduce the tracklayer and handler to tracklaying.
- Introduce the handler to lead handling.

Tracklayer:
- Study the tracklayer's instructions for session 1.1.
- Lay a pretend track like track 1.1.3 (the third track of phase 1, session 1) without a dog.
- Make sure you pick out a distant landmark to walk towards when laying the track. This will help you walk in a straight line.
- Study the handler's instructions for session 1.1 so you can remind the handler what to do.
- Help the handler with the line-handling lesson below.

Handler:
- Study the tracklayer's instructions for session 1.1 so you can be sure that the tracklayer is laying the track correctly.
- Lay a pretend track like track 1.1.3 without a dog.
- Make sure you pick out a distant landmark to walk towards when laying the track. This will help you walk in a straight line.
- Study the handler's instructions for session 1.1.
- Have the tracklayer act the part of a dog. Clip a 20' lead onto his belt and have him walk down a road in front of you. Try different tensions until you know how good a firm gentle tension feels like. Your line should not flop around in the breeze and the "dog" should not have to strain to get you to follow along behind him. Have the "dog" move off the track. Raise your arm and increase the tension. Have the "dog" move from side to side as you practice your lead handling.
- Switch roles. You be the "dog" and let the tracklayer handle. Feel what firm gentle tension is like. Move off the track and have the handler raise his arm. Feel the tendency to swing back to the track as his arm goes up and the tension increases.
- Make sure you have all your equipment ready for the next session.

Evaluation:
- Even though you probably felt stupid doing all this without a dog, it is better to feel a little stupid and learn how to do something correctly than either to not learn it at all or to confuse your dog as you are learning it later.

Session 1.1

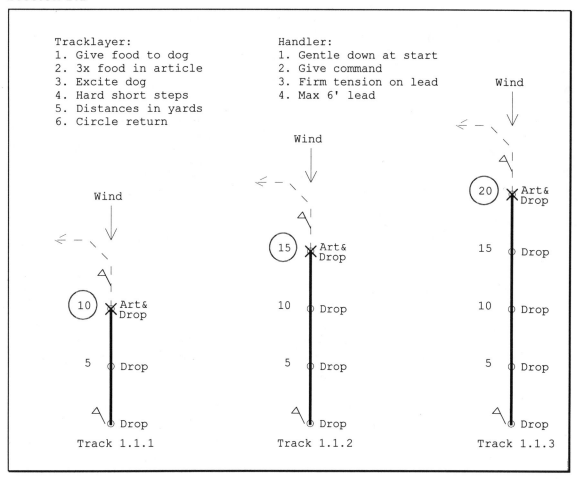

Tracklayer:
1. Give food to dog
2. 3x food in article
3. Excite dog
4. Hard short steps
5. Distances in yards
6. Circle return

Handler:
1. Gentle down at start
2. Give command
3. Firm tension on lead
4. Max 6' lead

Track 1.1.1   Track 1.1.2   Track 1.1.3

Purpose:
- Introduce the dog to tracking.
- Introduce the idea that when you give the command to track, there is something to find.
- Introduce the dog to the fun of tracking.

Tracklayer:
- At the start, place the first flag and choose the direction of the track directly into the wind.
- Turn 180° to face the dog.
- Ask in a happy voice if he wants to find the goodies today.
- While the handler restrains the dog, give him one piece of food.
- Have him watch you put three pieces of food into the article (put them in the article in a way to make it easy for him to get the food out of the article himself).
- Excite the dog with the article (don't worry if he does not get excited).
- Turn to face the direction of track.
- Leave a piece of food at the start between your feet.
- Make hard short steps (heel to toe) for five yards, all the while excitedly talking to the dog.
- Make a small footprint pad on the track, put a piece of food directly in the footprint pad, and tell the dog there are goodies out here.
- Proceed five more yards using hard short steps as before, continuing to talk to the dog.
- Make a small footprint pad, put the article with food in the footprint pad, and tell the dog that there is something exciting to find out here.

- Quietly walk two normal paces in the same direction and place a second flag right on the line of the track.
- Quietly walk a couple of more paces in the same direction, then start circling back to the dog. Stay 15 or more yards to the side of the track as you return.
- Walk behind the handler. Remind him to stay on the track and to keep good tension.

Handler:
- When you get to the start, put on the dog's harness and a six foot lead.
- Position dog a few feet from the start so he will look directly down the track as it is being laid.
- Restrain the dog so he can't quite get to the tracklayer, but so the dog can be given the food.
- Don't worry if the dog is not very interested in the proceedings, since he does not know what is going on yet.
- Try to gently keep the dog's attention on the tracklayer as the track is being laid.
- When the tracklayer returns, bring the dog up to the start holding the harness directly.
- Gently down the dog at the start if he is comfortable going down.
- Restrain him at the start until he smells and finds the food drop.
- Continue to restrain him at the start for a few seconds to give him a chance to start to sniff the footprints at the start.
- When he starts to sniff the footprints (or after a few seconds if he isn't going to actively sniff), give him your tracking command (such as "Find it!") and give him about 3 feet of lead.
- When he moves forward directly on the track, take a step.
- He is likely to cast widely from side to side. Don't worry at this stage, but only step along the track when he is on the track.
- Raise your hand with the lead over your head whenever the dog is off the track. Lower it whenever the dog is directly on the track. The height of your hand should be proportional to distance the dog is off the track. Belly high when he is right on the track.
- If he tends to move directly along track, let out more lead (up to six feet maximum).
- If he happens to go over the middle drop without eating it, restrain him there until he finds it. You do not need to praise him for finding the food drops.
- If he takes several steps straight down the track, praise quietly, but do not distract him.
- When he gets to the article, praise him wildly as soon as his nose comes close to the article.
- Help him get the food out of the article if necessary, excitedly play with him and the article, and give him some more food.
- Toss the article a very short distance and encourage him to go touch it or pick it up. Give him more food (on the article is good) and lots of praise. After the last track, play the article toss & touch game six to ten times.
- He should feel happy and proud of himself at the end of the track no matter what happened along the way! It is up to you to make him feel that way.
- Proceed to the next track to watch it being laid. Offer him water between tracks. After the third track, take off the harness before returning to the car.

Evaluation:
- Note in your tracking journal how he reacted to the proceedings. Did he sniff at the start or on the track? Did he smell, indicate, or play with the article? Did he stay on the track some of the time? Did he enjoy the food drops? Did anything happen to discourage him? Was he happy?
- If he used his nose at all, even for just an instant, you have had a very successful session. If not, don't worry. Many good tracking dogs take several sessions to get the idea. And he may have used his nose without you being aware of it.

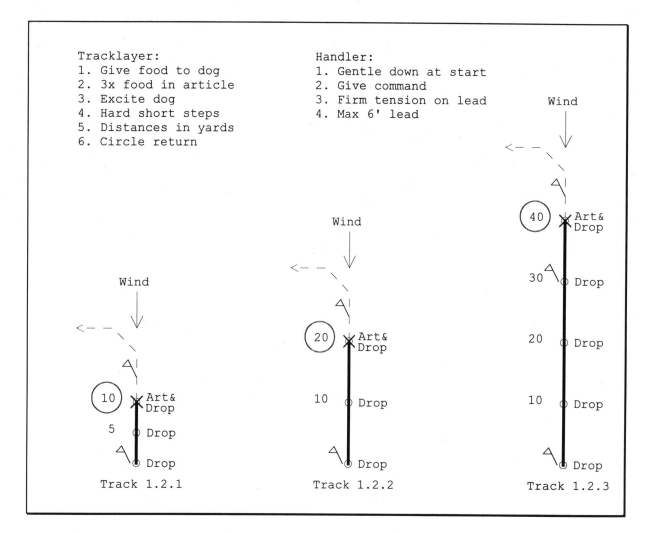

```
Tracklayer:                  Handler:
1. Give food to dog          1. Gentle down at start
2. 3x food in article        2. Give command
3. Excite dog                3. Firm tension on lead
4. Hard short steps          4. Max 6' lead
5. Distances in yards
6. Circle return
```

Track 1.2.1

Track 1.2.2

Track 1.2.3

Purpose:

o   See session 1.1.

Tracklayer:

•   Use distant landmarks to keep the tracks straight and into the wind.

•   Leave a second flag at 30 yards on every track that is longer than 30 yards.

o   See session 1.1.

Handler:

•   Work on improving your lead handling.

o   See session 1.1.

Evaluation:

o   See session 1.1.

Session 1.3

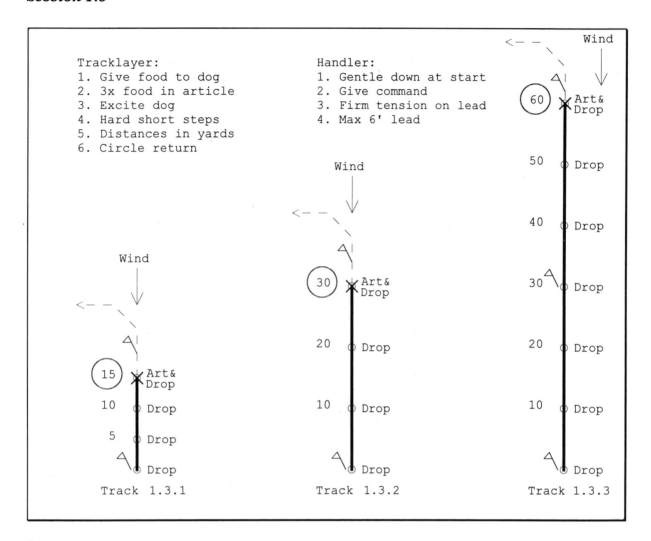

Tracklayer:
1. Give food to dog
2. 3x food in article
3. Excite dog
4. Hard short steps
5. Distances in yards
6. Circle return

Handler:
1. Gentle down at start
2. Give command
3. Firm tension on lead
4. Max 6' lead

Track 1.3.1

Track 1.3.2

Track 1.3.3

Purpose:

o   See session 1.1.

Tracklayer:

•   Keep up the enthusiasm when laying the track, even if the dog does not seem to be paying much attention.

o   See session 1.2.

Handler:

•   Keep working on your lead handling.

o   See session 1.1.

Evaluation:

•   Dog may be tracking several yards along the track at a time before being distracted.

•   Can you tell when dog is using his nose and when he is not?

o   See session 1.1.

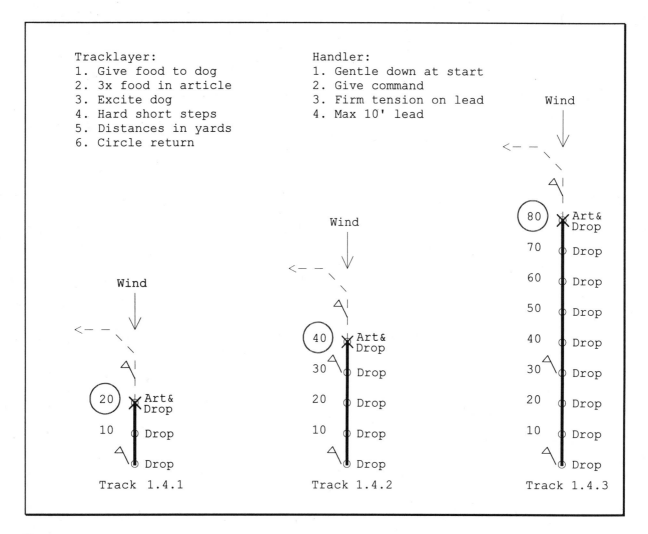

```
Tracklayer:                  Handler:
1. Give food to dog          1. Gentle down at start
2. 3x food in article        2. Give command
3. Excite dog                3. Firm tension on lead
4. Hard short steps          4. Max 10' lead
5. Distances in yards
6. Circle return
```

Track 1.4.1   Track 1.4.2   Track 1.4.3

Purpose:
o   See session 1.1.

Tracklayer:
o   See session 1.3.

Handler:
•   Extend lead length to 10' if dog seems to be getting the idea. Shorten it again if dog strays from the track too much of the time.

•   Start to gently insist on a particular style of article indication: touching, picking up, retrieving, sitting or downing.

o   See session 1.3.

Evaluation:
o   See session 1.3.

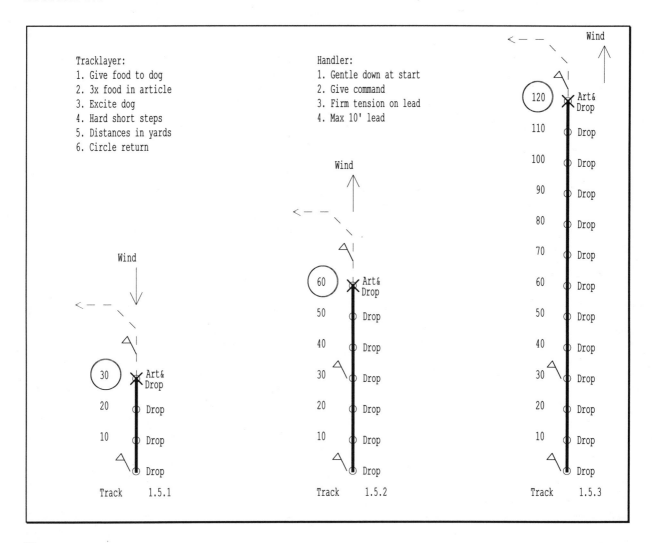

Tracklayer:
1. Give food to dog
2. 3x food in article
3. Excite dog
4. Hard short steps
5. Distances in yards
6. Circle return

Handler:
1. Gentle down at start
2. Give command
3. Firm tension on lead
4. Max 10' lead

Track   1.5.1

Track   1.5.2

Track   1.5.3

Purpose:
o   See session 1.1.

Tracklayer:
*   After the first track (which is into the wind) all tracks will be down wind. At the start of the second track, place the flag and choose the direction of the track directly down wind.
*   As the tracks get longer, use intermediate flags every 100 yards or so.
o   Otherwise, like session 1.1.

Handler:
*   The dog may act confused on first downwind track. Watch for the dog's nose coming down closer to the ground and for the dog to do less side to side casting.
o   See session 1.4.

Evaluation:
*   Notice how closely the dog is to the track and whether his nose is close to ground.
o   See session 1.3.

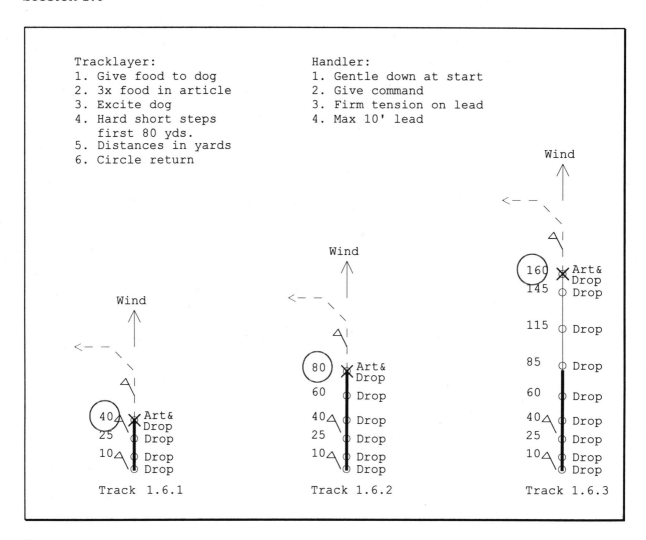

```
Tracklayer:                    Handler:
1. Give food to dog            1. Gentle down at start
2. 3x food in article          2. Give command
3. Excite dog                  3. Firm tension on lead
4. Hard short steps            4. Max 10' lead
   first 80 yds.
5. Distances in yards
6. Circle return
```

Track 1.6.1

Track 1.6.2

Track 1.6.3

Purpose:

• These tracks are doing more than introduce. They are teaching and the dog may be starting to learn.

o See session 1.1.

Tracklayer:

• The dog is probably paying less attention to you after you leave the start. Keep up the chatter and enthusiasm for at least the first 50 yards of each track.

o See session 1.5.

Handler:

• Watch for the dog's nose coming down closer to the ground and for the dog to do less side to side casting.

o See session 1.5.

Evaluation:

• Ideally, dog should be staying on track most of the way and indicating the article.

o See session 1.5.

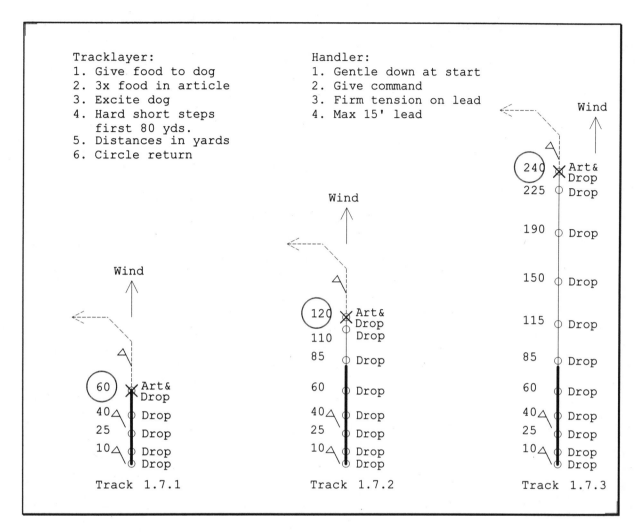

```
Tracklayer:                    Handler:
1. Give food to dog            1. Gentle down at start
2. 3x food in article          2. Give command
3. Excite dog                  3. Firm tension on lead
4. Hard short steps            4. Max 15' lead
   first 80 yds.
5. Distances in yards
6. Circle return
```

Track 1.7.1   Track 1.7.2   Track 1.7.3

Purpose:
o   See session 1.6.

Tracklayer:
- As tracks get even longer, be sure to use intermediate flags.
- If you have to bend the track slightly to get in the distance, it is OK; but use a flag there.
- If you can't get the whole distance laid, just stop rather than mess up the track doing something unusual that might confuse the dog. Bends up to 30° are OK.
o   See session 1.5.

Handler:
- Extend the lead length to 15' if dog is staying close to the track most of the time. Shorten it again if dog starts to stray from the track.
- Play the glove game with great enthusiasm. As the dog gets the idea, throw the glove farther.
o   See session 1.5.

Evaluation:
o   See session 1.6.

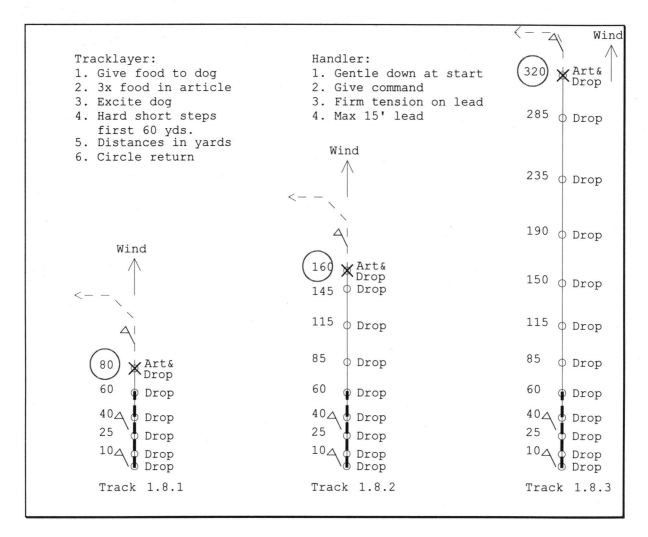

Tracklayer:
1. Give food to dog
2. 3x food in article
3. Excite dog
4. Hard short steps first 60 yds.
5. Distances in yards
6. Circle return

Handler:
1. Gentle down at start
2. Give command
3. Firm tension on lead
4. Max 15' lead

Track 1.8.1

Track 1.8.2

Track 1.8.3

Purpose:

o   See session 1.6.

Tracklayer:

·   As the tracks get long, be sure to use intermediate flags.

o   See session 1.7.

Handler:

•   Long tracks may cross changes in cover like a change from grass to weeds. Watch how the dog works at a change in cover. He may break off and have to find the track in the new cover.

o   See session 1.7.

Evaluation:

•   If dog is not indicating the article by now, start play training the dog with articles on non-tracking days. Throw the article, excitedly tell him to find it, and give the dog a treat as soon as his nose touches it. Repeat many times.

o   See session 1.7.

Session 1.9

Purpose:
* Review the dog's progress and summarize his accomplishments.

Evaluation:
* Don't expect either you or the dog to be perfect at this stage of the training.
* Write a summary of how your dog has tracked during this phase in your logbook.
* Write a review of his enthusiasm to start, his enthusiasm during the track, how close to the track he stays, how he reacts to changes in cover, and how he indicates the articles.
* Write down what you can do to encourage him to do better.
* Write a review of how well you show your enthusiasm for tracking during the training sessions, your lead handling ability, how the lead feels when your dog is tracking, how the lead feels when your dog is off the track, and how well you can read your dog when he is on or off the track.

Light Comfortable Tension – An Interlude

It may be unclear what is meant by the phrase *light comfortable tension*. I also use the phrase *firm tension* in the charts but this can be taken as synonymous with *light conformable tension*. Because tension is so important to your success as a dog-handler team, you need to establish good tension now to provide the proper foundation for your teamwork in phases 3 and above.

Individual dogs will consider different tensions light and comfortable. Picture what a 5-pound toy dog might consider as light comfortable tension. Then picture what a 90-pound sled dog might consider as light comfortable tension. These tensions are probably very different. The handler of the toy dog has the lead daintily between two fingers and there will be a slight arc in the line between the handler and the dog. The handler of the sled dog must wear gloves and is holding on to the line with all her might. She might even have the line wrapped around her waist. There is no arc in the line as the dog pulls the handler down the track. However, both of these tensions are *light comfortable tensions* for those individual teams. Your own dog is probably somewhere between these two extremes and so you will have to discover what your dog considers *light comfortable tension*.

In **all** cases, *light comfortable tension* involves tension! The line can never drag along the ground between the handler and the dog. The dog must be able to feel the presence of the handler by the tension in the line at all times. Any time the line goes slack or arcs too much, the dog loses contact with the handler and will either (1) look back to see what happened to the handler or (2) lose confidence and slow down. Neither of these actions is desirable. When the slack is taken up, the dog will feel a pop much like an obedience correction. So train yourself to maintain a light comfortable tension at all times while the dog is tracking.

In **no** case should the normal tension while the dog is right on the track be so high as to make the dog fight just to move forward. The comfortable part means that the tension is comfortable for the dog. The light part is important because you will increase the tension when the dog moves off the track.

Fast Dogs – A Related Interlude

The big dog that loves to pull and loves to run fast can present a dilemma to the handler. How can the tension be light and comfortable when the handler has to hold on for dear life? One part of the answer is that comfortable refers to the comfort of the dog and not the comfort of the handler. Sorry!

On the other hand, a handler should never let the dog pull so fast or so hard that the handler is in danger of falling or getting hurt. If the dog wants to go faster than the handler can safely follow, the handler must increase tension to slow the dog down and give the dog an "Easy" command. "Easy" means to slow down but to continue tracking. In slowing the dog down while he is on the track, you want to do so evenly without jerking or stopping the dog. It will be helpful to teach an "Easy" command on-lead in a non-tracking situation; then the dog will understand what "Easy" means so it can be useful on the track.

When a handler cannot safely keep up, some big fast dogs adopt a circling behavior to pass the time as the handler catches up and allows them to continue. Every 20 to 50 yards along the track, the dog breaks off tracking for no apparent reason and starts to circle wildly. This may be due to some jerking on the line, boredom, or just playfulness on the part of the dog. Treat it as an indication that your line handling should improve – you want the dog tracking steadily down the track. So, work on your "Easy" command and work on making your line handling smooth and even. Your dog will be much easier to read and the two of you will be a more successful team.

Phase 2. Developing Line Tracking Skills.

Purpose:
- Skill improvement for the dog and the handler.
- Age scent to 15 minutes.

Strategy:
- Return to very short tracks where the dog is frequently rewarded and finds the article quickly.
- Extend the length of the tracks and the distance between the rewards gradually.
- All tracks are laid downwind so the dog will stay on the track and not quarter over the track.
- Gradually increase the lead length as the dog starts to stay right on the track.
- Gradually increase the track age.
- Keep the dog unstressed and happy.

Schedule:

Session	Number of Tracks	Age Minutes	Track 1 Length	Track 2 Length	Track 3 Length	Total Length	Lead Length
2.1	3	5	10	15	20	45	6'
2.2	3	5	10	20	40	70	10'
2.3	3	8	15	30	60	105	15'
2.4	3	8	20	40	80	140	20'
2.5	3	10	30	60	120	210	20'
2.6	3	10	40	80	160	280	20'
2.7	3	15	60	120	240	420	20'
2.8	3	15	80	160	320	560	20'
2.9	Review						

Discussion:

Dog should be kept away from the start of the track. The dog is not to be excited by the tracklayer.

The tracklayer can lay two or three of these tracks in a row before returning to the start of the first to allow the dog to start.

Continue to practice play retrieves with the articles after the session and on non-tracking days. A highly motivated tracking dog may be so track oriented that it ignores the article. Maintaining a joyful glove game keeps a balance between the enthusiasm for the track and the enthusiasm for the articles.

Lead handling is very important and is worth reviewing. When the dog is exactly on the track, keep a light firm tension on the line with your hand at belly level. As the dog moves to the side, raise your hand gradually until it is over your head and increase the tension on the line. The further off the track the dog is, the higher your hand and the greater the tension. When the dog gets six feet off the track, your hand should be over your head and you should not be moving. Wait until the dog swings back toward the track, lowering your arm and the tension as he approaches the track, and take a step forward as he comes to the track. You are making it easy for the dog to stay on the track and hard to stray from the track.

You should have practiced that up and down lead handling all during phase 1. A further refinement will improve your technique and your dog's training. Whenever you hold the lead at belly level, use your arm as a shock absorber by holding your elbow out away from your body and your forearm square across your belly. As your dog suddenly pulls forward, your hand can automatically go forward with him keeping the light firm tension constant. As your hand is going forward, your body has an extra split second to speed up and stay with your dog. And as your dog suddenly slows down or stops, your hand can automatically pull back into your belly keeping the light firm tension constant. Your other hand holds the trailing line and can feed line forward or reel line back as the distance between you and your dog dynamically varies on the track. (Most right-handed people, like me, use their right hand as the lead hand. Left-handed people, I am told, always use the appropriate hand without needing advice.)

So on straight legs, you need only to remember to raise and lower your hand as the dog moves to the side of the track, and to use your arm as a shock absorber to maintain a steady light firm tension of the line.

Some people with very fast moving dogs, very slow moving dogs, very big dogs, or very small dogs think that they can be less careful about lead handling than other people. All this discussion about lead handling must be for someone else. In fact, careful lead handling is required for all dogs. Of course, the tension level for a big fast moving dog that loves to pull will be higher than the tension level for a small slow moving toy dog. But all dogs should have a steady tension without the lead flopping around in the breeze, without the lead touching the ground between the dog and handler, and without the dog being inadvertently jerked (corrected) by rapid changes in tension.

Handlers of small dogs may be able to handle the tracking line between their thumb and forefinger. Handlers of large dogs may have to wear thin gloves and wrap the line around the palm of their hand to hold the proper tension. Handlers of fast moving dogs may have to adjust to changes in speed more quickly to avoid slack and jerk. Handlers of all types of dogs will be better handlers if they adopt the lead handling style described above. It takes practice, but it is worth the effort.

Some students have noted that the tracks at the end of the first phase were older than five minutes, so perhaps they should age these tracks longer or even skip most of this phase. I applaud such creative thinkers but it turns out to be a bad idea. Follow the program as closely as you can and your dog will be a better and more successful tracker as a result.

To get ready for the next phase, practice corners with a 40-foot lead with another person acting the part of the dog. Lead handling on corners requires lots of practice. Also, study your dog's posture while it is tracking. Over the next several phases, you will improve your ability to read your dog as he is tracking and searching for the track.

Puppies: If you started a young puppy and scaled all distances in the first phase, you may choose to scale distances in this phase also. A high-energy puppy that is barreling his way down the track may well be old enough now to do full distances. A low-energy puppy or one who is not yet sure of himself should benefit from shorter distances. Do all the tracks in this phase. In phase three and beyond, you will work full distances with all dogs.

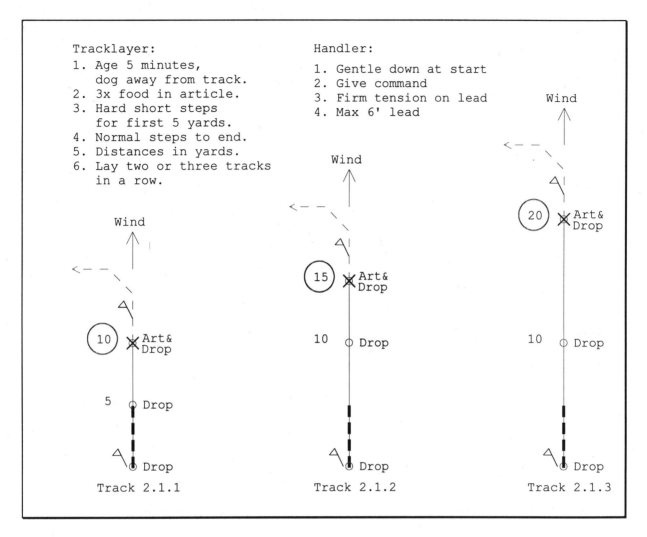

Tracklayer:
1. Age 5 minutes, dog away from track.
2. 3x food in article.
3. Hard short steps for first 5 yards.
4. Normal steps to end.
5. Distances in yards.
6. Lay two or three tracks in a row.

Handler:
1. Gentle down at start
2. Give command
3. Firm tension on lead
4. Max 6' lead

Track 2.1.1

Track 2.1.2

Track 2.1.3

Purpose:
- Give dog some easy tracks to increase motivation after long tracks in session 1.8.
- Introduce the dog to following tracks he has not seen laid.

Tracklayer:
- Lay out two or three tracks in a row, then circle return to meet dog and handler at start.
- Walk behind the handler on the track.

Handler:
- Keep dog away from tracks until they are laid.
- Bring the dog to within 10 yards of the first start and put on harness.
- Gradually raise your arm when dog moves off the track. Your arm should be over your head when the dog is six feet off the track. Lower it to belly level when he is on the track.
- Lots of enthusiasm when dog finds the article. Play with the dog and article at end of each track.

Evaluation:
- Note how dog tracks, indicates article, and level of enthusiasm for the tracks.

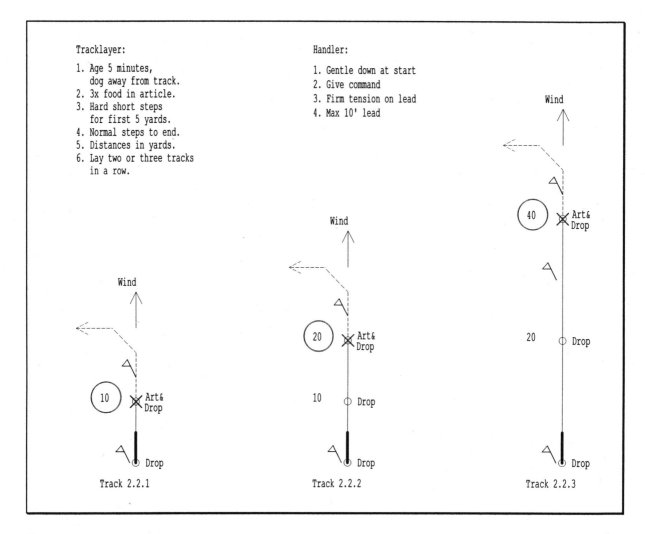

Tracklayer:

1. Age 5 minutes,
   dog away from track.
2. 3x food in article.
3. Hard short steps
   for first 5 yards.
4. Normal steps to end.
5. Distances in yards.
6. Lay two or three tracks
   in a row.

Handler:

1. Gentle down at start
2. Give command
3. Firm tension on lead
4. Max 10' lead

Track 2.2.1   Track 2.2.2   Track 2.2.3

Purpose:
o   See session 2.1.

Tracklayer:
•   Use distant landmarks to keep the tracks straight.
•   Leave a second flag at 30 yards on every track that is longer than 30 yards.
o   See session 2.1.

Handler:
•   Work on improving your lead handling.
•   Keep playing the glove game after every track.
o   See session 2.1.

Evaluation:
o   See session 2.1.

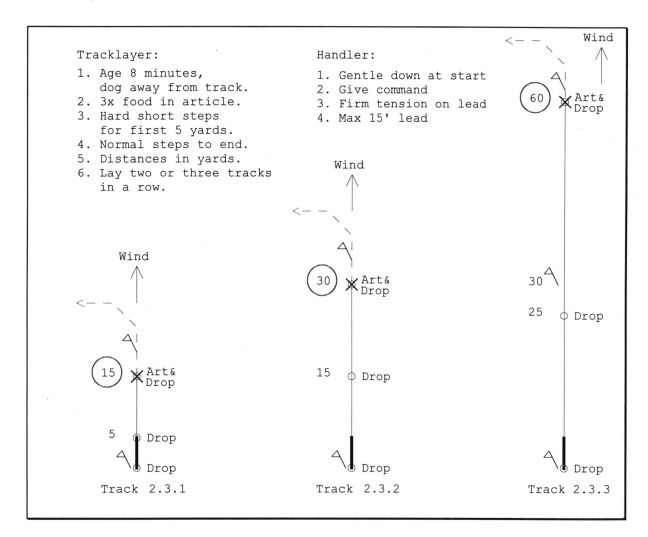

Tracklayer:
1. Age 8 minutes,
   dog away from track.
2. 3x food in article.
3. Hard short steps
   for first 5 yards.
4. Normal steps to end.
5. Distances in yards.
6. Lay two or three tracks
   in a row.

Handler:
1. Gentle down at start
2. Give command
3. Firm tension on lead
4. Max 15' lead

Track 2.3.1

Track 2.3.2

Track 2.3.3

Purpose:
o   See session 2.1.

Tracklayer:
o   See session 2.2.

Handler:
o   See session 2.2.

Evaluation:
o   See session 2.1.

Session 2.4

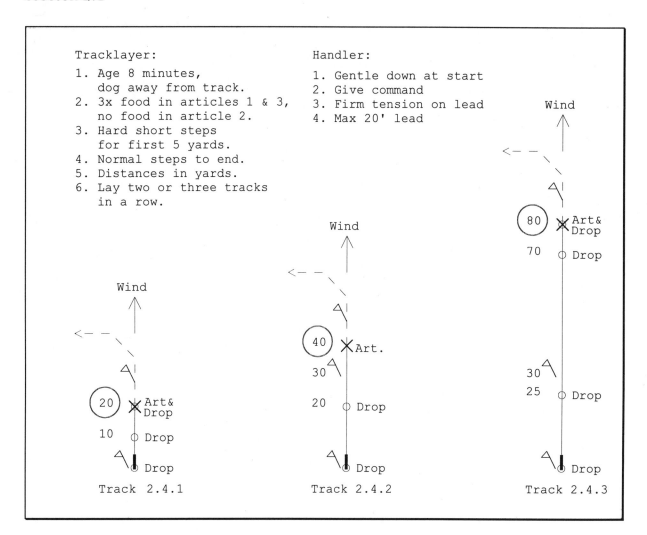

Tracklayer:
1. Age 8 minutes,
   dog away from track.
2. 3x food in articles 1 & 3,
   no food in article 2.
3. Hard short steps
   for first 5 yards.
4. Normal steps to end.
5. Distances in yards.
6. Lay two or three tracks
   in a row.

Handler:
1. Gentle down at start
2. Give command
3. Firm tension on lead
4. Max 20' lead

Wind

80 ✗ Art&
       Drop
70 ○ Drop

30 ⌐
25 ○ Drop

   ○ Drop

Track 2.4.3

Wind

40 ✗ Art.
30 ⌐

20 ○ Drop

   ○ Drop

Track 2.4.2

Wind

20 ✗ Art&
       Drop
10 ○ Drop

   ○ Drop

Track 2.4.1

Purpose:
*   Introduce dog to articles without food.
*   Improve the dog's tracking concentration and skill.
o   See session 2.1.

Tracklayer:
*   If dog has been indicating articles with food, leave no food in the second article.
o   See session 2.2.

Handler:
*   Handler should move up line as the dog approaches the article without food and immediate give food and wild praise when the dog indicates the article. Don't let the dog walk over article, restrain at article until the dog indicates it in any way, then food and wild praise.
o   See session 2.2.

Evaluation:
o   See session 2.1.

Session 2.5

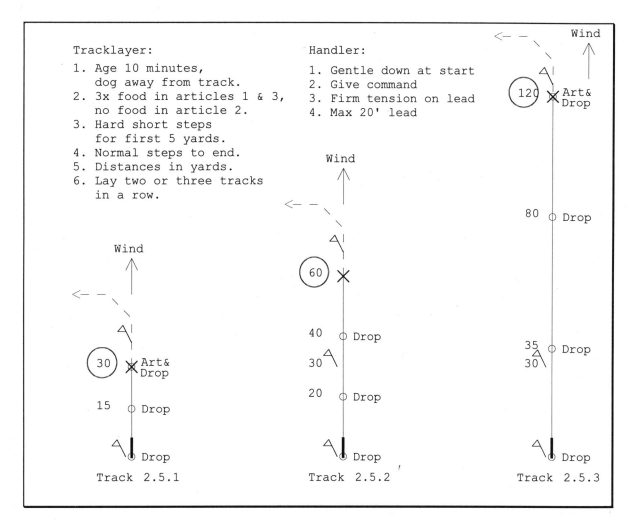

Tracklayer:

1. Age 10 minutes,
   dog away from track.
2. 3x food in articles 1 & 3,
   no food in article 2.
3. Hard short steps
   for first 5 yards.
4. Normal steps to end.
5. Distances in yards.
6. Lay two or three tracks
   in a row.

Handler:

1. Gentle down at start
2. Give command
3. Firm tension on lead
4. Max 20' lead

Wind

120 Art&
     Drop

80 Drop

35 Drop
30

Track 2.5.3

Wind

60

40 Drop

30

20 Drop

Drop

Track 2.5.2

Wind

30 Art&
    Drop

15 Drop

Drop

Track 2.5.1

Purpose:
o   See session 2.4.

Tracklayer:
o   See session 2.4.

Handler:
o   See session 2.4.

Evaluation:
•   Note how the dog handles articles without food.
o   See session 2.1.

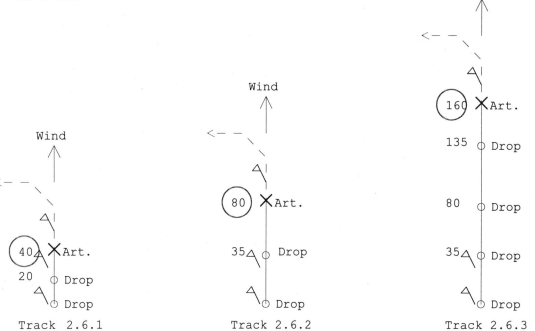

Tracklayer:
1. Age 10 minutes,
   dog away from track.
2. Food in articles optional.
3. Normal steps.
4. Distances in yards.
5. Lay two or three tracks
   in a row.

Handler:
1. Gentle down at start
2. Give command
3. Firm tension on lead
4. Max 20' lead

Wind

160 ✗ Art.

135 ⊙ Drop

80 ⊙ Drop

35 ⊙ Drop

⊙ Drop

Track 2.6.3

Wind

80 ✗ Art.

35 ⊙ Drop

⊙ Drop

Track 2.6.2

Wind

40 ✗ Art.

20 ⊙ Drop

⊙ Drop

Track 2.6.1

Purpose:
o   See session 2.4.

Tracklayer:
o   See session 2.4.

Handler:
o   See session 2.4.

Evaluation:
o   See session 2.5.

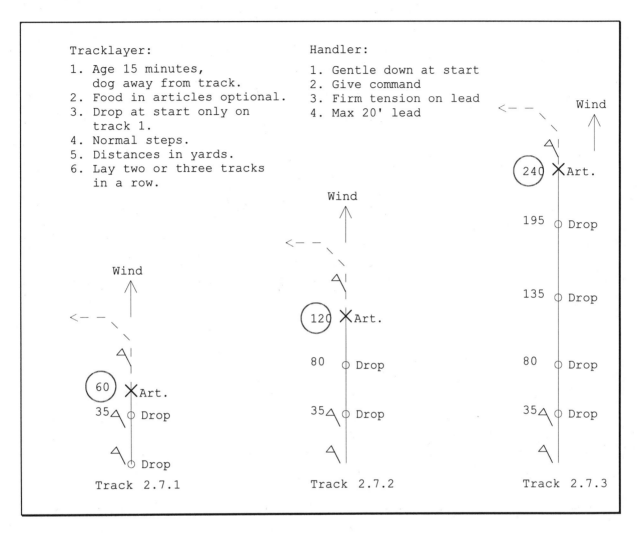

```
Tracklayer:                      Handler:
1. Age 15 minutes,               1. Gentle down at start
   dog away from track.          2. Give command
2. Food in articles optional.    3. Firm tension on lead
3. Drop at start only on         4. Max 20' lead
   track 1.
4. Normal steps.
5. Distances in yards.
6. Lay two or three tracks
   in a row.
```

Track 2.7.1

Track 2.7.2

Track 2.7.3

Purpose:
- Teach dog that a track can start without a food drop.
- See session 2.4.

Tracklayer:
- Leave off drops at the starts of tracks 2 and 3.
- As tracks get even longer, be sure to use intermediate flags.
- If you have to bend the track slightly to get in the distance, it is OK; but use a flag there.
- If you can't get the whole distance laid, just stop rather than mess up track doing something un-usual that might confuse the dog. Bends up to 30° are OK.
- See session 2.4.

Handler:
- See session 2.4.

Evaluation:
- See session 2.5.

Session 2.8

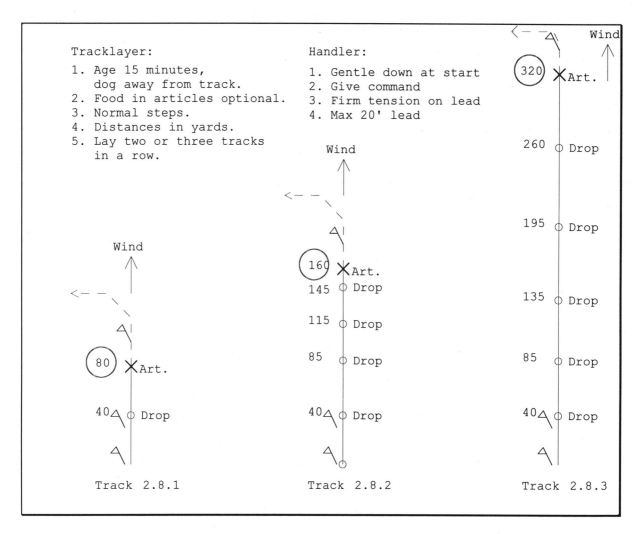

Tracklayer:

1. Age 15 minutes,
   dog away from track.
2. Food in articles optional.
3. Normal steps.
4. Distances in yards.
5. Lay two or three tracks
   in a row.

Handler:

1. Gentle down at start
2. Give command
3. Firm tension on lead
4. Max 20' lead

Track 2.8.1   Track 2.8.2   Track 2.8.3

Purpose:

o   See session 2.7.

Tracklayer:

•   As the tracks get long, be sure to use intermediate flags.
o   See session 2.7.

Handler:

•   Long tracks may cross changes in cover like a change from grass to weeds. Watch how the dog
      works at a change in cover. He may break off and have to find the track in the new cover.
o   See session 2.4.

Evaluation:

•   If dog is not indicating the article without food by now, play train the dog with articles on non-
      tracking days. Throw the article, excitedly tell him to find it, and give the dog a treat as soon as
      his nose touches it. Repeat many times.
o   See session 2.5.

Session 2.9

Purpose:
*   Review the dog's progress and summarize his accomplishments.

Evaluation:
*   Don't expect either you or the dog to be perfect at this stage of the training. However, your dog should be attentively tracking most of the lengths of the tracks.
*   Write a summary of how your dog has tracked during this phase in your logbook.
*   Write a review of his enthusiasm to start, his enthusiasm during the track, how close to the track he stays, how he reacts to changes in cover, and how he indicates the articles.
*   Write down what you can do to encourage him to do better.
*   Write a review of how well you show your enthusiasm for tracking during the training sessions, your lead handling ability, how the lead feels when your dog is tracking, how the lead feels when your dog is off the track, and how well you can read your dog when he is on or off the track.

Walking in a Straight Line – A Tracklayer's Interlude

When laying some of the long tracks in the first two phases you will have noticed how hard it is to walk in a straight line for several hundred yards. The straighter you walk, the easier time you will have if the dog gets lost and you have to help the handler find the track. Also, if you walk in a straight line, the dog and handler will have an easier time and will be more successful – so you will be a popular tracklayer.

The easiest way to walk in a "perfectly" straight line is to notice two landmarks in the distance that are lined up with the direction you want to go but that are in fact well separated from each other. Say you are going to lay a 200-yard straight track in a field, at the far edge of the field is a large fence post, and directly behind that fence post is a telephone pole in the far distance. If you keep these two landmarks lined up as you walk towards them, you will walk in a straight line.

Often you will be unable to find such convenient landmarks in the direction you want to go. Perhaps you can find one but there is no second landmark in line with the first. If you look carefully, you may notice a tuft of grass or a unique weed in the foreground that lines up with the main landmark. Use this foreground landmark until you get close to it, and then find another clump of grass or weed that is in line with the main landmark. This technique is more difficult because you have to use several landmarks along the one straight leg, but it can keep you in a relatively straight line.

Finally, on hilly terrain, you may lose sight of your landmarks as you go up and down the slopes. Use several intermediate landmarks on this type of leg, choosing your next landmark before you get to the current landmark or before it goes out of view.

If you have to bend a leg that the handler expects to be straight, put in an extra flag at the bend to avoid confusion and to help the handler as she is following her dog.

Improvisation – Another Tracklayer's Interlude

Always try to do exactly what the handler asks you to do. Get the handler to write down exactly what you should do and clarify any issue before you start to lay the track. No matter how careful you are, unexpected situations will arise as you are laying the track and you will be called upon to do something. Here are some rules that you should keep in mind as you are improvising:

- If the situation seems hopeless, drop an article, put in a flag, and return to the handler and tell her what happened. If the handler does not want to run the dog on the track as laid, someone else might have a dog ready for it or you can always enjoy walking the track again to pick up the flags and the article.
- If you have a choice between two or more alternatives, choose the simplest alternative that will make the track easier rather than harder for the dog and handler. Tell the handler what you did.
- If anything about the track makes it more difficult than the handler expects, put down additional food treats five to ten yards past the difficulty to reward the dog for getting past the obstacle. Tell the handler what you did.
- If you do not have an article, use a sock, a hat, a handkerchief, a tee shirt, a belt, or whatever you can spare. Do not use your keys, your wallet, your eyeglasses, or anything valuable since it might be stolen by a passerby, destroyed by the dog when he finds it, or never found again.

Phase 3. Introduce Corners.

Purpose:

- Teach crosswind tracking.
- Teach right and left turns.

Strategy:

- Keep dog on track on crosswind legs.
- Allow dog to overshoot corner a small distance.
- Allow dog to investigate the corner area.
- Encourage dog to take new leg quickly.

Schedule:

Session	Configuration	Track 1 Downwind	Track 2 Crosswind	Track 3 Upwind	Track 4 Crosswind	Total Length
3.1	Big Square	75	75	75	75	300
3.2	Big Square	75	100	75	100	350
3.3	Big Square	100	100	100	100	400

Session	Turns	Wind	Track 1 Leg 1	Track 1 Leg 2	Track 2 Leg 1	Track 2 Leg 2	Track 3 Leg 1	Track 3 Leg 2	Total Length
3.4	Right	into	100	20	100	40	100	80	440
3.5	Left	into	100	20	100	40	100	80	440
3.6	Right	into	125	60	125	160			470
3.7	Left	with	125	60	125	160			470
3.8	Right	with	140	80	160	160			540
3.9	Left	with	160	125	200	200			685
3.10	Review								

Overview:

Up until now, we have always tracked directly into the wind or directly downwind. Since we cannot lay a track with a 90° corner where both legs go directly with the wind. One of the legs must be a crosswind leg. So before we introduce a dog to his first corner, we introduce the dog to crosswind tracks in the first three sessions of this phase. In these three sessions, we lay four separate tracks in a big square so the dog must track in four different wind directions on the same day. The tracks in the remaining six sessions each have one corner. We want the second leg of these tracks to be a familiar type of track so it will be easy for the dog to take the second leg. This means the second leg should be an upwind leg, making the first leg a crosswind leg.

Crosswind Tracking

In a crosswind, the dog will tend to track a few feet downwind of the footsteps. This is natural, but can easily become a bad habit. You should raise your arm and increase the tension in proportion to how far he is off the track. If he stays off the track, you can move upwind of the footsteps up to 3' to increase the torque helping to bring him back on the track. Now is a critical time to keep the dog close to the footsteps. Care now can avoid problems later. Remember, our strategy is to make it easiest for the dog to move forward directly over the footsteps and to make it more difficult to move forward when the dog is off the track.

Don't expect the dog to be perfect in the crosswind on his first track. How far he wants to track off the footsteps depends on the wind strength, track age (15 minutes), weather and his experience. As he gains positive experience tracking in a crosswind, he will become a solid crosswind tracker. He will be doing well if, in the first few tracks, he moves parallel to the track within 3 feet of the footsteps. But he must be under increased tension while off the footsteps any distance, so keep your arm up and a nice firm tension. By the middle of this phase, he may be happily tracking right on the footprints with only an occasional diversion downwind.

During sessions 2 and 3, we add angle starts to introduce the dog to the idea that the track may not be right in front of you and him. Expect the dog to burst forward when you release him at the start. Because of the angle, this will cause him to diverge from the track. Increase the tension, keep the dog from diverging more than 6 feet, and remind him to find it. Give him a few seconds to circle over to find the track. If he doesn't, point to the track and happily encourage him to find the track.

Avoiding Problems

The food drops become less frequent in this phase. You may notice the dog picks up speed and stays closer to the track after the drops. That's why they are there. You may notice him going off the track downwind a few yards before the drops. This is normal since there is a lot of scent near the drops. If you cross a cover change or other slight obstacle that the dog has not experienced before, put a drop five paces past the obstacle. The drop will properly reward the dog for getting past the obstacle.

If he is not starting well, go back to putting a drop at the start and another at 15 yards. Withdraw these two extra drops slowly and randomly once his enthusiasm returns.

If the dog is losing enthusiasm near the end of the track, do two things: a) condition him on non-tracking days to improve his stamina, and b) increase the number of food drops on the last half of the track.

The Ideal Corner

Before discussing what a dog is going to do on his very first corner, let's understand what we would like him to do once he is experienced with corners. Ideally, when a dog comes to a corner, he immediately turns his head down the new leg and marches around the corner like a cartoon character bending around a corner. Alternatively, if he is moving down the leg quickly when he comes to the corner, he should nod his head down the direction of the new leg, put on the brakes and quickly come to a stop within a few feet of the corner. When he does pass the corner, the ideal dog will immediately and actively search for the new direction by circling until he intersects and takes the new leg.

Many dogs, including those who nod in the direction of the new leg as they go past the corner, seem to want to check out the opposite direction before taking the new leg. They may circle to the opposite direction, then come up to the corner and proceed down the new leg. Let the dog search however he wants to search, so long as it is active and purposeful. How a dog circles may be influenced by his innate tendency to turn right or left, the wind direction, tracking conditions, and his drive to continue on the track.

The First Corner

A good deal of what we did in the first two phases is to develop a strong drive to complete the track so the dog is ready to handle corners.

Every dog is different, but you should expect to see some typical behavior when the dog reaches his first few corners. Since the dog has been tracking the footprints, and has always found a glove, he has never run out of scent before. So expect him to continue down the line of the first leg for several feet before realizing that the track has been lost. Two to three body lengths past the corner might be typical depending on how fast he is moving. At the instant he runs out of scent, he may look back at you with a puzzled expression. Perhaps he is saying "No fair, you've changed the rules of the game!".

Some dogs immediately start to look for the track while others are less sure what to do. It does not really matter because we are going to teach the dog to search for the track by our actions at the corner. Since we are about 15 feet behind the dog when he notices the loss of track, we are not quite to the corner flag when we stop. The handler stays were he stops 15 feet behind the dog, smiles, and happily says his tracking word "Find it!". If the dog does not stop within 5-10 feet past the corner, increase the tension until the dog stops, and stop yourself before the corner.

Be ready to raise your arm over your head to avoid getting the line tangled with the dog, or the stake, or vegetation. Some handlers like to keep their arm straight over their head the whole time they are on a corner. I prefer to keep the lead in both hands at chest level, constantly adjusting the lead length to control the dog's distance from me and raising my arm only when it is necessary to avoid tangling the line.

Continue to face the direction of the first leg while noting the footprints and flags of the second leg. You want to encourage the dog to find the direction of the second leg without, if possible, helping him find it. By keeping your body facing down the direction of the first leg, you avoid giving the dog clues about what direction to search. You want him to understand that he is the one doing the searching. Do keep a steady comfortable tension on the line and quietly encourage the dog to "Find it. Go ahead. You can do it. That's right, find it."

Watch how the dog's nose works as he approaches the track (or directly downwind of the track). When the dog reaches the second leg, he will generally start right out on the upwind leg. Some dogs seem to notice the second leg but are reluctant to take it. An upwind leg probably smells a little different from a crosswind leg, so he may not be sure it is the same track. Feel free to encourage him to take the leg if he does not take it or even show him the new leg if he can't find it. Just give him a chance to find it himself before helping him.

If the dog needs help, first encourage him with your voice and your body language to go in the correct direction. If he still needs help, reach down and tickle the grass right on the track right in front of his nose as you happily encourage him to find it. Walk forward with him down the track tickling the track until he takes off ahead of you. It is important to maintain a happy attitude whenever you help your dog.

See the Corner Problems section below for a discussion of how to train dogs who tend to overshoot the corners, who want to play on the corner, and dogs who want to quit on a corner.

The Second Leg

When the dog takes the second leg, you may notice him weaving from side to side. This is natural on an upwind leg. A dog that weaved on the upwind legs of Phase 1 will probably weave on these upwind legs also. Of course, you want to encourage him to stay right on the track by raising your arm and increasing the tension in proportion to how far off the track he is.

On subsequent corners in this phase's tracks, your dog will gain understanding about corners and how to work them. Keep the image of the ideal corner in your mind and encourage his behavior that is close to the ideal.

Corner Problems

You can avoid extensive problem solving later by watching for and intervening when you first see consistent signs of a corner problem.

1. **Line Tracking.** Some dogs tend to track a considerable distance past the corner. We call these dogs "line trackers" since they like to keep going in a line. To discourage this behavior from developing, don't let the dog get 20' past the corner. Stop when you are 5' from the corner and increase the tension until the dog stops within 20' of the corner. Proceed as described above. If the problem seems to persist, build tracking drive by putting drops at 25, 30 and 35 yards past each corner. Escalate to drops at 25, 30, 35, 40 and 45 if needed.

2. **Playing.** Some dogs want to play at the corner - as soon as they run out of scent, they take it as permission to run wildly about having a good time. We try to keep this from happening by building tracking drive in the dog during the first two phases, using quiet encouragement for the dog to search on the corner and using steady tension on the line at the corner. Dogs that start to play should have the line tension increased and have drops at 25, 30 and 35 yards past the each corner. A dog that persists in playing should have several remedial straight tracks in various wind conditions until he is a happy tracker in all wind directions. You can repeat session 3.1 with four straight 75 yard tracks that make a box shape by laying one track into the wind, the next crosswind, the next downwind, and the next back crosswind. Start each track about 10 yards from the end of the previous track. Then try a corner session again. If the dog plays on the corners again, do several more four-square sessions. This time use a motivational food pattern to encourage the dog to complete the track. On a 75-yard track, put food at the start, 15, 40, 55, 65 and 70 yards.

3. **Confusion.** The occasional dog does not seem to get the idea that the track might make a corner and acts confused at nearly every corner. Even after completing all of phase three, he continues to act lost on each corner and does not seem to adopt any search tactics. When he happens to come upon the next leg (say by chance or after some encouragement), he tracks it but acts just as confused the next time he comes to a corner. Dogs who lack self-confidence are susceptible to confusion on corners.

I have found gradual corners a good way to retrain such dogs. Over a set of five sessions, introduce slight bends in the track and gradually make them sharper until the dog is handling 90° corners. The turns should be "randomly" to the left and right. However, the second leg must always be exactly upwind for the first four sessions. This means you must plan the direction of the first leg so that a turn of the correct angle will be directly upwind. In session GT5, the second leg of all tracks is exactly downwind. Then sessions 3.7-3.9 are repeated with their last legs downwind. So for the first four sessions, the dog will do gradual turns exactly upwind followed by four sessions with the second leg exactly downwind.

Session	Track 1			Track 2			Track 3			Total
	Leg1	Angle	Leg2	Leg 1	Angle	Leg 2	Leg 1	Angle	Leg 2	Length
GT.1	75	165	40	100	150	60	100	135	80	455
GT.2	75	150	40	100	135	60	100	120	80	455
GT.3	75	135	40	100	120	60	100	105	80	455
GT.4	75	120	40	100	105	60	100	90	80	455
GT.5	75	120	40	100	105	60	100	90	80	455
Repeat 3.7	125	90	60	125	90	160				470
Repeat 3.8	140	90	80	160	90	160				540
Repeat 3.9	160	90	125	200	90	200				685

If the dog starts to act confused during this set of sessions, repeat a session or go back a session or two. You want to see the dog act with confidence before proceeding to the next phase of training.

4. **Quitting.** Some dogs may become perplexed when they lose the scent at the corner. They may stop, look at you and not actively search. Alternatively, they may look for a while and then become discouraged when they cannot immediately find it. (Dogs that lack self-confidence are prone to this problem). Wait a moment when the dog first stops to see if he will restart on his own. If not, repeat your tracking command "Find it". Then repeat your extended tracking command "Search for it. Go ahead. You can do it. Find it." Be happy, take a few steps toward the corner, and repeat the extended command.

If the dog does not get started again, reduce the lead length to a few feet and walk down the second leg with the dog while pointing at the footsteps and happily and excitedly saying "Look over here. Here it is. You can do it. You can find it." Encourage the dog down the track until he moves out in front of you. He will soon find a drop and the article, so he will quickly understand that these new legs are OK.

Dog who quit also can benefit from the gradual turn sessions described above. They are used to build confidence.

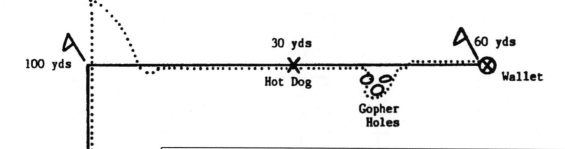

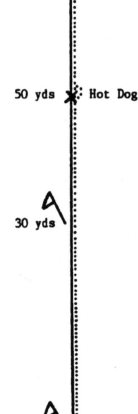

Tracking from the Dog's Point of View

The frosty morning air chills my nose as I pull Pops into a field. The dew wets my legs and drips from my beard as I scamper through the tall grass. Sniff-sniff, the scents that rise to my nose as the sun warms the field tell a story of mice and deer that crossed this way last night. However, I cannot tarry to hunt, since we have come to the starting flag and Pops is putting on my tracking harness.

Now Pops likes to take this tracking business more seriously than I do. Don't get me wrong; I love to follow the footsteps, find the hotdogs along the way, and nuzzle the glove at the end that is ever so full of goodies. However, Pops likes me to stay right on the track the whole way. Sometimes there are aromas just screaming to be investigated! Moreover, occasionally the footsteps simply disappear - I think they try to trick me sometimes - and I forget what scent I am supposed to follow. I digress too much, let's get back to the track...

Pops downs me at the flag which someone has tramped around. The strong odor of the tracklayer mixes with that of the crushed grass as it drifts to my nose. I struggle to get up and start down the track which lies in front of me, but Pops holds me down a few more seconds before finally freeing me.

I dash down the first leg of the track a few yards when I feel the reassuring tension of the tracking line. I lean into the harness a little to tell Pops I know where I am going. Soon I hear him clumping along behind me. What with my water canteen clanking against his leg, he can make enough of a din out here to drown out the birds chirping in the trees ahead. We are making pretty good time when all of a sudden a bit of hot dog passes under my nose - "STOP! STOP!" I tell my body, but I have to turn around and sniff it out. Sniff-sniff, a little to the left; sniff-sniff, just ahead; sniff-sniff, there it is! Yummy, this is so much fun!

Off we go again, down the footstep highway. I don't want to go quite so fast and miss any of the hot dogs. Sniff-sniff, where is the track now? It was just under my nose a few seconds ago. I stop and the clumping stops behind me. I lift my nose up to the top of the grass to try to scent where it went. There seems to be more floating over from the right, so I'll try to investigate over there. As I bound through the grass, Pops holds the line taut so I will circle the area. One more hop and the scent splashes in my face as I land by a footstep. Oh boy, I've found it again.

I charge forward a few steps, but the scent heads off to my left. I correct course, lean into the harness, and Pops is soon clumping along behind me. Sniff, there's a hotdog ahead! I pounce upon it and am off down the track in a split second.

Oh boy, gopher hole! I'll just catch some vermin while I'm here and get back to the track in just a minute. "NO MOUSES TODAY", Pops says. He can't mean that, it's gophers, not mice! "NO MOUSES TODAY!", he repeats. Well, I'd better appease him - the odor around the gopher hole is cold anyway - he does think he's boss although I know better.

Back to the track, now where did it go? Off to the left, by the smell of it. I dash over there and quickly cross it. Oh boy, this is easy. I tug Pops along behind me as the breeze blows the aroma of the article down to me. Sniff-sniff, it must be right around here somewhere. Sniff-sniff, the fragrance of hotdogs, and garlic, and chicken livers, and old leather overpower the whole area. Yippee, it is right here! Yummy, all these goodies just for me! Yahoo, Pops comes up with pets, praise, and even more goodies! This is so much fun!

Tracklayer

1. Lay 4 tracks in a
   large square.
2. Separate tracks by
   25-50 yards.
3. Normal pace on tracks.
4. Age 15 minutes.
5. Lay 4 tracks in a row.

Handler:

1. Keep dog on track.
2. Increase tension when
   dog is off track.
3. Approach the start of
   each track directly down
   the track.

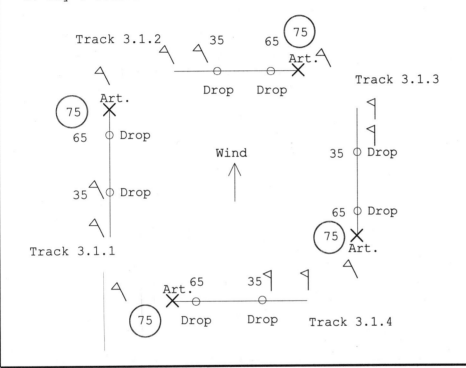

Purpose:
- Introduce crosswind legs.

Tracklayer:
- Lay four tracks in a big square; first one directly downwind (or upwind).
- Lay all the tracks in a row, keep 25-50 yards apart.

Handler:
- Keep the dog on the track.
- Increase the tension and raise your arm when dog goes off the track.
- Approach the start of each track directly down the track.

Evaluation:
- Note how dog works in each wind direction.

Tracklayer

1. Lay 4 tracks in a
   large square.
2. Separate tracks by
   25-50 yards.
3. Normal pace on tracks.
4. Age 15 minutes.
5. Lay 4 tracks in a row.

Handler:

1. Keep dog on track.
2. Increase tension when
   dog is off track.
3. Approach start of each
   track at a slight angle
   (about 30 degrees).

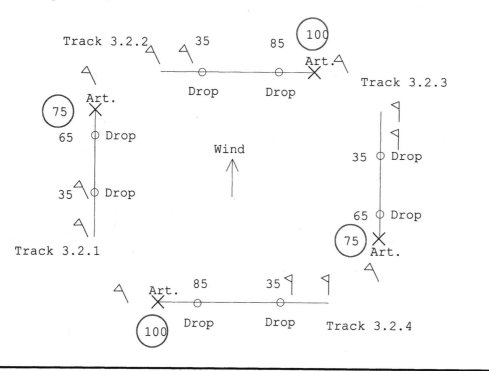

Purpose:
- Build confidence on crosswind legs.
- Angle starts introduces dog to pseudo-corners.

Tracklayer:
- Lay four tracks in a big square; first one directly downwind (or upwind).
- Lay all the tracks in a row, keep 25-50 yards apart.

Handler:
- Approach each start from a 30° angle (from right and left randomly).
- Keep the dog on the track.
- Increase the tension and raise your arm when dog goes off the track.

Evaluation:
- Note how dog works in each wind direction.

Session 3.3

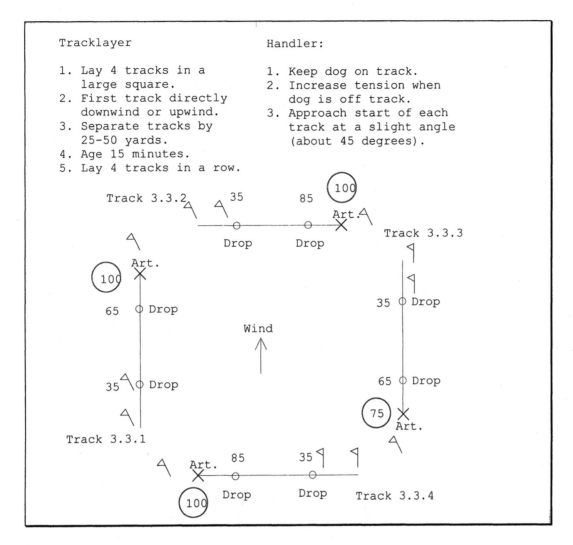

```
Tracklayer                      Handler:

1. Lay 4 tracks in a       1. Keep dog on track.
   large square.           2. Increase tension when
2. First track directly       dog is off track.
   downwind or upwind.     3. Approach start of each
3. Separate tracks by         track at a slight angle
   25-50 yards.               (about 45 degrees).
4. Age 15 minutes.
5. Lay 4 tracks in a row.
```

Track 3.3.2   35   85   100

Art.   Track 3.3.3

Drop   Drop

Art.   100   35   Drop

65   Drop   Wind

35   Drop   65   Drop

75   Art.

Track 3.3.1

Art.   85   35   Track 3.3.4

100   Drop   Drop

Purpose:
* Build confidence on crosswind legs.
* Angle starts introduces dog to pseudo-corners.

Tracklayer:
* Lay four tracks in a big square; first one directly downwind (or upwind).
* Lay all the tracks in a row, keep 25-50 yards apart.

Handler:
* Approach each start from a 45° angle (from right and left randomly).
* Keep the dog on the track.
* Increase the tension and raise your arm when dog goes off the track.

Evaluation:
* Note how dog works in each wind direction.

```
Tracklayer                      Handler:

1. Lay second leg into wind.    1. Keep dog on track on first leg.
2. Short Hard Step second leg.  2. Let dog up to 10' past corner.
3. Normal pace on first leg.    3. Let dog investigate corner area.
4. Age 15 minutes.              4. When dog investigates second leg,
5. Lay 2 or 3 tracks in a row.     lower tension to encourage.
                                5. As dog moves out on second leg,
                                   increase tension before you move
                                   off the corner.
```

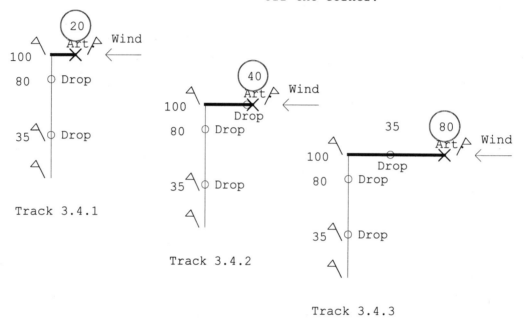

Purpose:
*   Introduce right turns.
*   Practice crosswind legs.

Tracklayer:
*   Lay second leg into wind with short hard steps.
*   Extend your arms at the corners to sight landmarks at 90 degrees.
*   Use four flags per track so handler will know exactly where track is laid.
*   Lay two or three tracks in a row, keep 50 yards apart.

Handler:
*   Keep 15' behind dog as you approach the corner.
*   Stop yourself before the corner.
*   Encourage the dog to search and find new leg.
*   Face down the direction of the first leg until the dog commits to the next leg or needs help.

Evaluation:
*   Note how dog works the corners. Also note how he maintains his attitude on each leg.

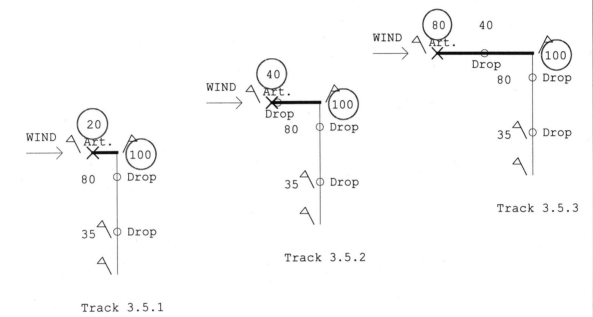

Tracklayer

1. Lay second leg into wind.
2. Short Hard Step second leg.
3. Normal pace on first leg.
4. Age 15 minutes.
5. Lay 2 or 3 tracks in a row.

Handler:

1. Keep dog on track on first leg.
2. Let dog up to 10' past corner.
3. Let dog investigate corner area.
4. When dog investigates second leg, lower tension to encourage.
5. As dog moves out on second leg, increase tension before you move off the corner.

Track 3.5.1

Track 3.5.2

Track 3.5.3

Purpose:
- Introduce left turns.
- Practice crosswind legs.

Tracklayer:
- Use distant landmarks to keep the tracks straight.
- Left turns upwind.
- o   See session 3.4.

Handler:
- Keep good tension on the line at corner.
- Work on improving your lead handling.
- o   See session 3.4.

Evaluation:
- o   See session 3.4.

```
Tracklayer                        Handler:

1. Lay second leg into wind,      1. Keep dog on track on first leg.
   short hard step first 20 yds.  2. Let dog up to 15' past corner.
2. Normal pace on first leg.      3. Let dog investigate corner area.
3. Age 15 minutes.                4. When dog investigates second leg,
4. Lay both tracks in a row.         lower tension to encourage.
                                  5. As dog moves out on second leg,
                                     increase tension before you move
                                     off corner.
```

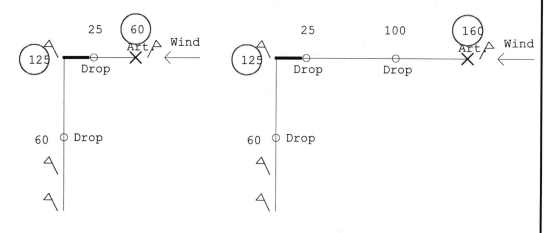

Track 3.6.1   Track 3.6.2

Purpose:
* Practice corners and crosswind legs.

Tracklayer:
* Right turns upwind.
o See session 3.4.

Handler:
* Keep 20' behind dog as he approaches the corner.
o See session 3.5.

Evaluation:
o See session 3.4.

Tracklayer

1. Lay second leg WITH wind, short hard step first 20 yds.
2. Normal pace on first leg.
3. Age 15 minutes.
4. Lay both tracks in a row.

Handler:

1. Keep dog on track on first leg.
2. Let dog up to 15' past corner.
3. Let dog investigate corner area.
4. When dog investigates second leg, lower tension to encourage.
5. As dog moves out on second leg, increase tension before you move off corner.

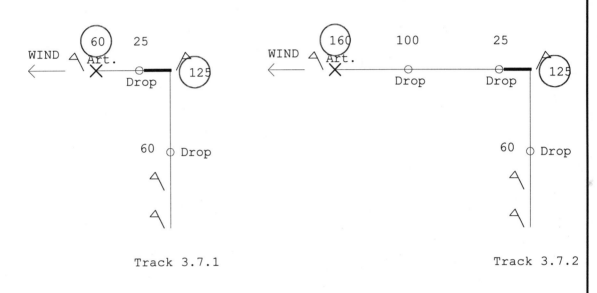

Track 3.7.1   Track 3.7.2

Purpose:

o   See session 3.6.

Tracklayer:

•   Left turns downwind.

o   See session 3.6.

Handler:

o   See session 3.6.

Evaluation:

o   See session 3.4.

Tracklayer

1. Lay second leg with wind, short hard step first 20 yds.
2. Normal pace on first leg.
3. Age 15 minutes.
4. Lay both tracks in a row.

Handler:

1. Keep dog on track on first leg.
2. Let dog up to 20' past corner.
3. Let dog investigate corner area.
4. When dog investigates second leg, lower tension to encourage.
5. As dog moves out on second leg, increase tension before you move off corner.

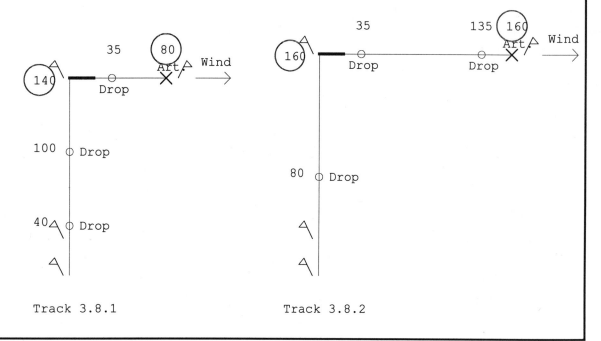

Track 3.8.1   Track 3.8.2

Purpose:

o   See session 3.6.

Tracklayer:

•   Right turns downwind.
o   See session 3.6.

Handler:

o   See session 3.6.

Evaluation:

o   See session 3.4.

Session 3.9

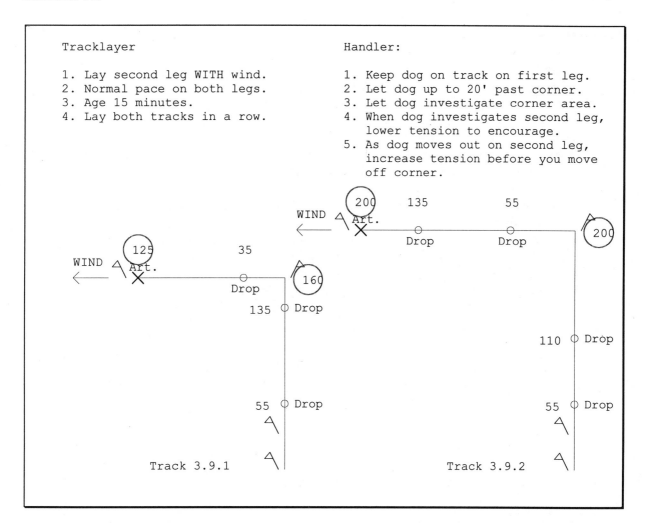

Tracklayer

1. Lay second leg WITH wind.
2. Normal pace on both legs.
3. Age 15 minutes.
4. Lay both tracks in a row.

Handler:

1. Keep dog on track on first leg.
2. Let dog up to 20' past corner.
3. Let dog investigate corner area.
4. When dog investigates second leg, lower tension to encourage.
5. As dog moves out on second leg, increase tension before you move off corner.

Track 3.9.1

Track 3.9.2

Purpose:
o   See session 3.6.

Tracklayer:
•   One Right and one Left turn, both downwind.
o   See session 3.6.

Handler:
o   See session 3.6.

Evaluation:
o   See session 3.4.

Session 3.10

Purpose:
- Review the dog's progress.
- Summarize his accomplishments.

Evaluation:
- Don't expect to be a perfect handler at the corners yet. However, your dog should be enthusiastically tracking the legs and taking the corners with little problem.
- If your dog is typically confused on corners or is regularly quitting at corners, use the Gradual Turn sessions shown below. A dog that is handling most of the corners correctly does not need these sessions.
- Write a summary of how your dog takes corners, how you handle him at the corners, and how to read him when he is past a corner and when he has taken the second leg.
- Write a review of his enthusiasm to start, his enthusiasm during the track, his enthusiasm on the corners, how close to the track he stays, how he reacts to the corners, and how he indicates the articles.
- Write down what you can do to encourage him to do better.

Gradual Turn 1

(Use these sessions only if necessary. See text above on Corner Problems, Confusion.)

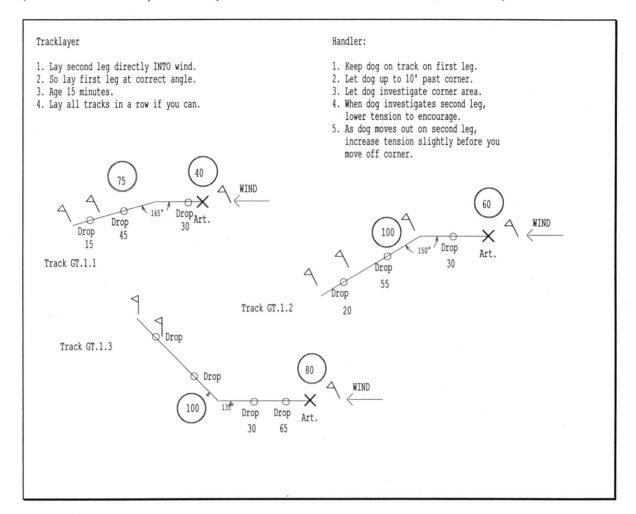

Purpose:
* Reintroduce turns.

Tracklayer:
* Lay second leg exactly into the wind.
* Aim first leg to allow the specified turn angle to bring you directly upwind.
* Use four flags per track so handler will know exactly where track is laid.
* Lay two or three tracks in a row, keep 50 yards apart.

Handler:
* Keep 15' behind dog as you approach the corner.
* Stop yourself before the corner.
* Encourage the dog to search and find new leg.
* Face down the direction of the first leg until the dog commits to the next leg or needs help.

Evaluation:
* Note how dog works the corners and how he maintains his attitude on each leg.

Gradual Turn 2

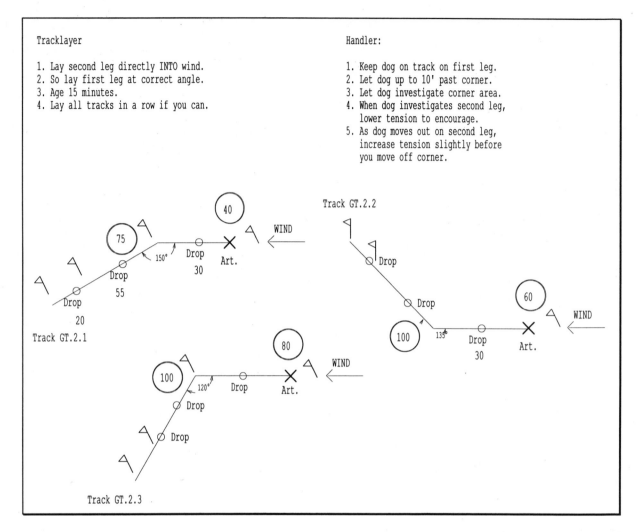

Tracklayer

1. Lay second leg directly INTO wind.
2. So lay first leg at correct angle.
3. Age 15 minutes.
4. Lay all tracks in a row if you can.

Handler:

1. Keep dog on track on first leg.
2. Let dog up to 10' past corner.
3. Let dog investigate corner area.
4. When dog investigates second leg, lower tension to encourage.
5. As dog moves out on second leg, increase tension slightly before you move off corner.

Purpose:
*   Reintroduce turns.

Tracklayer:
*   Lay second leg exactly into the wind.
*   Aim first leg to allow the specified turn angle to bring you directly upwind.
*   Use four flags per track so handler will know exactly where track is laid.
*   Lay two or three tracks in a row, keep 50 yards apart.

Handler:
*   Keep 15' behind dog as you approach the corner.
*   Stop yourself before the corner.
*   Encourage the dog to search and find new leg.
*   Face down the direction of the first leg until the dog commits to the next leg or needs help.

Evaluation:
*   Note how dog works the corners and how he maintains his attitude on each leg.

Gradual Turn 3

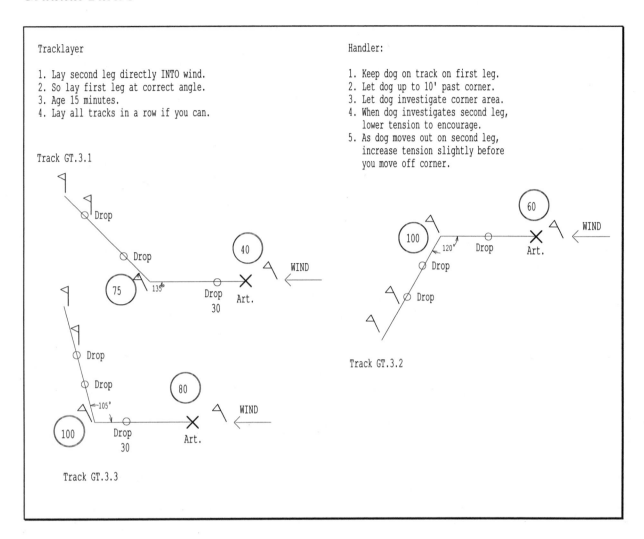

Tracklayer

1. Lay second leg directly INTO wind.
2. So lay first leg at correct angle.
3. Age 15 minutes.
4. Lay all tracks in a row if you can.

Track GT.3.1

Track GT.3.2

Track GT.3.3

Handler:

1. Keep dog on track on first leg.
2. Let dog up to 10' past corner.
3. Let dog investigate corner area.
4. When dog investigates second leg, lower tension to encourage.
5. As dog moves out on second leg, increase tension slightly before you move off corner.

Purpose:
* Reintroduce turns.

Tracklayer:
* Lay second leg exactly into the wind.
* Aim first leg to allow the specified turn angle to bring you directly upwind.
* Use four flags per track so handler will know exactly where track is laid.
* Lay two or three tracks in a row, keep 50 yards apart.

Handler:
* Keep 15' behind dog as you approach the corner.
* Stop yourself before the corner.
* Encourage the dog to search and find new leg.
* Face down the direction of the first leg until the dog commits to the next leg or needs help.

Evaluation:
* Note how dog works the corners and how he maintains his attitude on each leg.

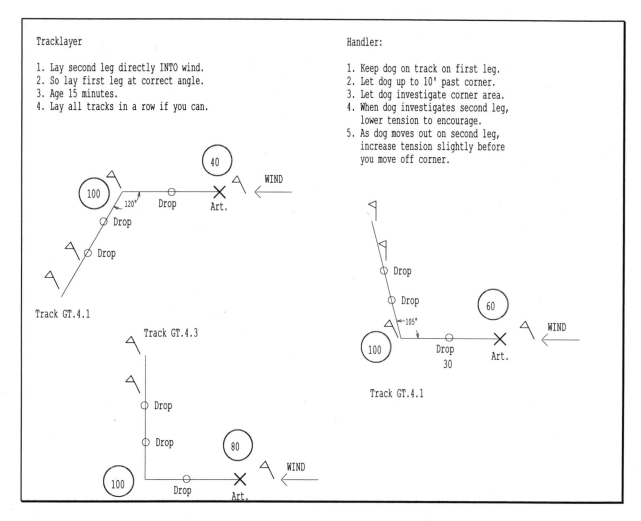

Tracklayer

1. Lay second leg directly INTO wind.
2. So lay first leg at correct angle.
3. Age 15 minutes.
4. Lay all tracks in a row if you can.

Handler:

1. Keep dog on track on first leg.
2. Let dog up to 10' past corner.
3. Let dog investigate corner area.
4. When dog investigates second leg, lower tension to encourage.
5. As dog moves out on second leg, increase tension slightly before you move off corner.

Purpose:
• Reintroduce turns.

Tracklayer:
• Lay second leg exactly into the wind.
• Aim first leg to allow the specified turn angle to bring you directly upwind.
• Use four flags per track so handler will know exactly where track is laid.
• Lay two or three tracks in a row, keep 50 yards apart.

Handler:
• Keep 15' behind dog as you approach the corner.
• Stop yourself before the corner.
• Encourage the dog to search and find new leg.
• Face down the direction of the first leg until the dog commits to the next leg or needs help.

Evaluation:
• Note how dog works the corners and how he maintains his attitude on each leg.

Gradual Turn 5

Tracklayer

1. Lay second leg directly WITH wind.
2. So lay first leg at correct angle.
3. Age 15 minutes.
4. Lay all tracks in a row if you can.

Handler:

1. Keep dog on track on first leg.
2. Let dog up to 10' past corner.
3. Let dog investigate corner area.
4. When dog investigates second leg, lower tension to encourage.
5. As dog moves out on second leg, increase tension slightly before you move off corner.

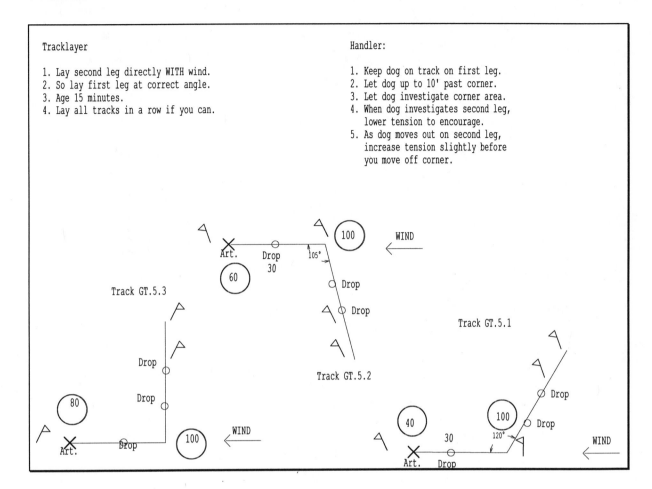

Purpose:
- Reintroduce turns.

Tracklayer:
- Lay second leg exactly with the wind.
- Aim first leg to allow the specified turn angle to bring you directly downwind.
- Use four flags per track so handler will know exactly where track is laid.
- Lay two or three tracks in a row, keep 50 yards apart.

Handler:
- Keep 15' behind dog as you approach the corner.
- Stop yourself before the corner.
- Face down the direction of the first leg until the dog commits to the next leg or needs help.

Evaluation:
- Note how dog works the corners and how he maintains his attitude on each leg.

Phase 4. Multiple Corners.

Purpose:

•   Practice right and left turns on same track.
•   Practice crosswind tracking.
•   Learn to read dog.

Strategy:

•   Keep dog on track.
•   Allow dog to overshoot corner a small distance.
•   Allow dog to investigate corner area.
•   Encourage dog to take new leg quickly.
•   Watch the dog's posture and the way he scents when he is on the track and off the track.

Schedule:

Session	Track 1 Leg 1	Track 1 Leg 2	Track 1 Leg 3	Track 2 Leg 1	Track 2 Leg 2	Track 2 Leg 3	Total Length
4.1	100	75	25	100	100	50	450
4.2	100	75	25	100	100	50	450
4.3	100	100	75	125	125	100	625
4.4	100	100	75	125	125	100	625
4.5	100	100	75	125	125	100	625
4.6	100	100	75	125	125	100	625
4.7	Review						

Discussion:

These tracks introduce the dog to tracks with multiple corners and give the dog and handler practice with corners under a variety of conditions.

After 14 tracks with a single corner, some dogs are confused by the second corner. You've changed the rules of the game again. However, they quickly learn this new, more complex game and become comfortable with tracks with multiple corners.

These sessions come in pairs, with the first track first turning left one session and first turning right the other session. Feel free to switch these sessions within pairs if it makes it easier to layout the two tracks in your fields. In some fields, you can start the second track within 25 yards of the first. Just keep the legs at least 50-yards apart.

Review the discussion about corners from phase 3 before proceeding. If you are seeing consistent signs of line tracking, playing, or quitting, reassess your handling and training technique and consider the gradual turn sessions as discussed in phase 3.

Reading Your Dog

This is the last phase when the tracks are clearly marked by stakes and flags. You need to notice how your dog acts when he is right on the track, a little bit off the track, and when he has lost the scent. How he holds and moves his head and nose, the arch of his back, the position of his tail, and how he pulls into the harness are all signals that can be read by the handler. Some dogs hold their head low to the ground and move their nose from footprint to footprint, creating a side to side swing of the head. Other dogs hold their head much higher, sniffing the scent as it rises off the ground. Some dogs hold their tail up when on the track, some hold it straight back and others hold it down between their legs.

It is important for you to learn your dog's posture and actions:
- when he is tracking,
- when he is off the track,
- when he runs out of scent at a corner,
- and when he finds and commits to the next leg.

Each day, note in your journal what signs you are able to read in your dog.

Reading the Landscape

You will also find it useful to learn to read the landscape so you have a better idea of where you are in the field. The first step in reading the landscape is to note a landmark in line with the leg you are on so that when the dog loses scent at the next corner, you can stay oriented in the field as the dog searches for the subsequent leg.

Practice the first step in reading the landscape by looking over your dog after it has committed to a new leg and note the landmark ahead of the dog. Probably, the tracklayer used this same landmark. You can confirm this landmark by also noting that the next corner flag is in line with the dog and landscape as well.

Communication on the Corner

It is essential that you develop a consistent means of communication with your dog on corners. We have discussed one aspect of that communication: reading your dog. There is another equally important aspect that will help you out of many difficult situations. That aspect is to build a means to double-check that your dog is taking the correct track after a corner.

On a blind corner where you cannot see where the corner is or where the new leg goes, it is natural to be a little uncertain that the dog is correct. Since you will be facing blind corners in the next phase, it is time to start developing this corner communication while you still have flags to reassure yourself that all is well.

A system of communication that works very well consists of this sequence of steps:
* Your dog clearly indicates loss of track within a few yards of the actual corner.
* You read your dog's behavior, recognize the loss of track and stop.
* Your dog purposefully searches for the new leg while you maintain a light comfortable tension with no slack. Your dog notices the new leg as it is searching and follows it a few feet.
* You increase the tension slightly and verbally ask the dog "Is this the good track?"
* Your dog leans into the harness.
* You *immediately* decrease the tension back to your normal light-comfortable tension, step out behind the dog, and praise your dog quietly.
* Your dog receives a reward a short distance down the new leg.

Communication is a two way process. Both you and your dog have important things to communicate to the other. Your dog tells you about the track scent by his actions. You communicate your questions and confidence through slight adjustments in line tension.

This system of corner communication works so well because the skilled dog will invariably veer off a false track it is investigating when reminded to stay on the good track. Therefore, if the dog does not veer off the line it is taking, you have great confidence that it is on the original good track. You communicate your confidence to the dog quickly, which strengthens its self-confidence. Now if the dog is distracted even a few yards further along the track, say by a deer crossing or another scenting difficulty, you are both ready to handle this new situation. Without this type of communication, you will be still uncertain about the new track direction when the subsequent distraction confounds the situation.

Work on this process of corner communication while the flags are still up and there is always a food drop 30-40 yards past the corner to reward the dog for pulling into the harness when you question him. Avoid jerking the line when you increase the tension and ask the question. Some dogs may be initially put off by even this gentle increase in tension, but you will happily encourage them to continue on down the new leg and they will learn it is just something that you do on corners.

Wind Direction

It is preferable to lay these tracks with the first leg going upwind. However, careful wind control is less a priority in this phase and future phases than it was in the first three phases. Start these tracks into the wind if you can, but don't worry about it if you cannot.

Typical tracking behavior of a dog tracking in several different wind directions is illustrated in the figure below. The wind is blowing from the top of the page to the bottom for all four tracks shown. A particular dog's path is shown by the curving lines.

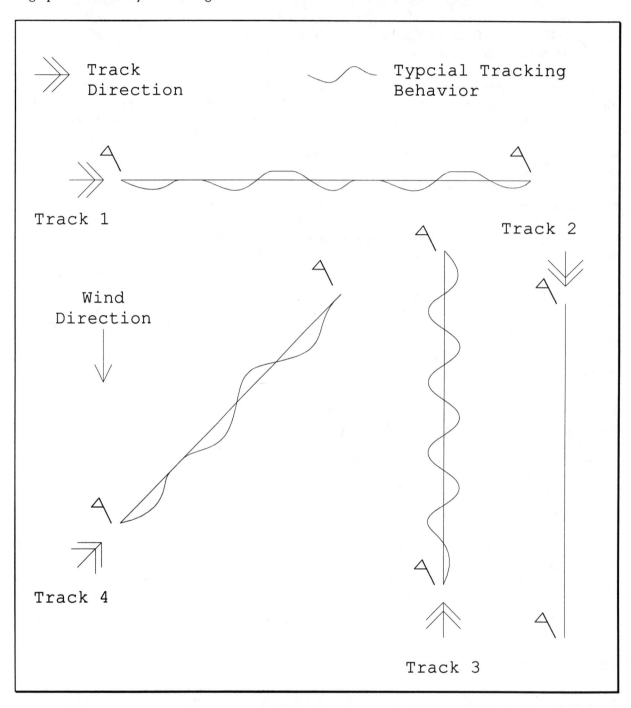

Track 1 is laid in a 90° crosswind. The dog tends to be blown downwind of the track. He may naturally come back to the track and track there a while before being blown downwind again. In some conditions, he may even track upwind of the track.

Track 2 is laid directly downwind. Most dogs who have been trained to stay close to the track will be quite good about staying right on top of a downwind leg.

Track 3 is laid directly upwind. Many dogs will cast from side to side while tracking upwind as shown by the wavy lines. They may follow the swirling scent that is coming downwind from the track ahead or they may attempt to detect differences in scent strength.

Track 4 is laid at a 45° angle upwind. Dogs tend to show a combination of the tracking behavior on upwind and crosswind tracks on such angled tracks.

It is important to understand these wind-directed tracking behaviors so you can recognize them in the field and train your dog to stay right over the footsteps. You train by raising your arm and increasing the tension when the dog is off the track. The height of your arm and the amount of tension are proportional to the distance the dog is off the track. You want to make it easy for the dog to track right on the track, somewhat difficult for the dog to track three-feet off the track, and impossible for the dog to track six-feet off the track. This line tension contrast in combination with the frequent food rewards that occur right on the track will tend to make the dog track close to the footsteps. This is also the most reliable place to track.

If you allow the dog the freedom to track ten to twenty feet off the track, your dog will learn that it can follow the track out there by detecting subtle differences in scent strength along the fringe of the scent coming from the track. However, such fringe followers do not make reliable trackers, because the swirling eddies make the fringe a very complex and difficult place to track. In addition, it is much easier to read a dog that is tracking in a straight line than it is to read one tracking a fringe. So it is best to teach the dog that no matter how good a fringe follower he might be, he will be a better tracker and have the easiest time by staying right over the footsteps. Moreover, you will be able to read his tracking behavior much more easily when the flags come down. Then you will not know where the track goes and you will have to read your dog to know when he is on the track and when he is having difficulty finding it.

With proper training, your dog should stay much closer to the tracks than the figure above illustrates. However, even a well trained dog can be blown off the track when other conditions such as track age or terrain make the scenting difficult for the dog.

Scent Phenomena

Although people cannot smell nearly as well as a dog can smell, observant handlers can learn a lot by watching their dog's behavior in different conditions. I will point out some phenomena to look for, the dog behavior commonly associated with it, and a training behavior you should adopt when it happens with your dog.

1. Scent tends to pool in low areas. Dogs may be drawn off a track into depressions of various sizes. These pools probably smell just like the track, so it is hardly a mistake for the dog to check it out. Allow your dog to briefly check out the pool, then happily encourage him to continue on the good track even if you have to point it out to him.

2. Scent rises as the sun warms the meadow. You will often see a dog track up-slope of the track on a windless sunny morning. Treat it like a crosswind – make it fun to stay right on the track.

3. Scent falls downhill. Without the sun warming the air and causing it to rise, one tends to see a dog tracking down-slope of a track. Again, treat it like a crosswind – make it fun to stay right on the track.

4. Scent hangs along fences and brush lines. When a track goes hear a fence or brush line, you may see the dog go over to the fence or brush and act like he is tracking over there. As with scent pooling in

low areas, allow your dog to check it out, but then happily encourage him to continue right on the track. Your dog is likely to become unreliable if he is allowed to follow the irregular fringe line of the scent.

5. The track ages faster in hot dry weather than in cool damp weather. Dogs act like the scent is fainter or harder to find in hot dry weather unless they are already used to it. Be extra careful to run your tracks at the specified time in hot-dry weather. If it is unusually hot and dry, run the track a little younger than specified.

6. Different vegetation affects how the tracks smell. Dogs tracking in one type of vegetation, such as grass, break off the track at a transition to a different type of vegetation, such as weeds. They notice the difference in scent and search around for the original track. This is good. You have to teach them that the track in the weeds is the same as the one in the grass. Teach this by first always putting an extra food drop 10 to 20 yards past a change in vegetation. Then allow him to search by himself for a short while. If the dog does not commit to the leg in the new vegetation, happily help and encourage him to do so.

7. Scent is swept away from the top of hills. Dogs tracking over the crest of a ridgeline or knoll of a hill tend to lose the track there and need to search for it again. Perhaps the microclimate of the knoll causes the vegetation to be different or sparser than the surrounding hillside. Perhaps the geometry of the knoll allows the wind to sweep much of the scent away. With enough practice, dogs do learn to track over a knoll, but it is clearly more difficult for them than flat areas. Train for knolls and ridgelines just like changes in vegetation above.

8. Scent is pushed away from tree lines. If a track parallels a tree line close to the trees, dogs will sometimes track well away from the trees and the track. John Barnard, the AKC Executive Field Representative for Tracking, does an excellent demonstration with smoke bombs that shows why this might happen. As a first approximation, the turbulence caused by the tree line causes the scent to swirl as far out into the field as the trees are tall. Therefore, the dogs that track away from the tree line may be really tracking the scent that has been swirled away from the track. In training, treat this just like a crosswind and keep your dog close to the track.

Watch for these and other behaviors in your dog while it is tracking. Being familiar with them can help you better read your dog on a blind track. For example, on a blind track, if my dog tracked down a hill and then lost the track, I must be willing to back up farther up the hill to find a corner than if it was a perfectly level area. Understanding these phenomena also helps with training. For example, knowing that it is "normal" for a partially trained dog to track poorly on an over-aged track on a hot day, you can help the dog quickly and freely in this unfortunate situation. You also know that the next track should be younger than normal and easier than normal to maintain the dog's motivation to track.

Tracklayer

1. Lay first leg into wind.
2. Short Hard Step 20 yds of second & third legs.
3. Normal pace on first leg.
4. Keep tracks 50 yards apart.
5. Age 15 minutes.
6. Lay both tracks in a row.

Handler:

1. Keep dog on track on all legs.
2. Let dog up to 10' past corner.
3. Let dog investigate corner area.
4. When dog investigates next leg, lower tension to encourage.
5. As dog moves out on next leg, increase tension before you move off the corner.

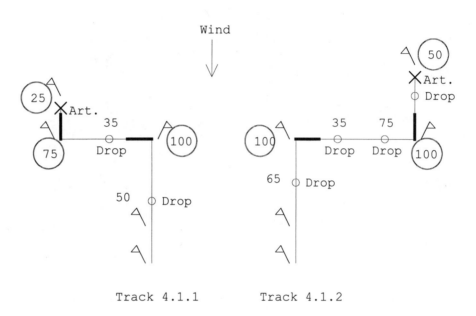

Track 4.1.1   Track 4.1.2

Purpose:
- Introduce two turn tracks and practice crosswind tracking.

Tracklayer:
- Make a map of these tracks as you lay them and include landmarks.
- Lay the first 20 yards of the second and third legs with short hard steps.
- Extend your arms at the corners to sight landmarks at 90 degrees.
- Use five flags per track so handler will know exactly where track is laid.

Handler:
- Stop before corner.
- Keep good tension on line at corner. Practice Corner Communication Process.
- Encourage the dog to search and find new leg.

Evaluation:
- Note how the dog works the corners and how he maintains his attitude on each leg.
- Note how you are reading your dog - what signs indicate he is on or off the track.

Session 4.2

```
Tracklayer                              Handler:

1. Lay first leg into wind.             1. Keep dog on track on all legs.
2. Short Hard Step 20yds of             2. Let dog up to 10' past corner.
   second  & third legs.                3. Let dog investigate corner area.
3. Normal pace on first leg.            4. When dog investigates next leg,
4. Keep tracks 50 yards apart.             lower tension to encourage.
5. Age 15 minutes.                      5. As dog moves out on next leg,
6. Lay both tracks in a row.               increase tension before you move
                                           off the corner.
```

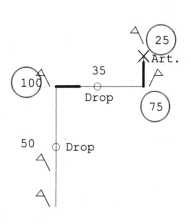

Track 4.2.1

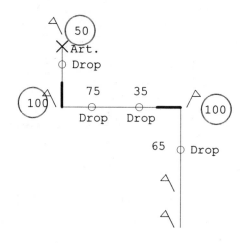

Track 4.2.2

Purpose:
o   See session 4.1.

Tracklayer:
•   Use distant landmarks to keep the track legs straight.
o   See session 4.1.

Handler:
•   Work on reading your dog.
•   Practice Corner Communication Process.
•   Remember to play the glove game after every track.
o   See session 4.1.

Evaluation:
o   See session 4.1

Tracklayer

1. Disregard wind unless dog
   is having problems.
2. Short Hard Step first 20 yds
   of third leg.
3. Normal pace on first two legs.
4. Keep tracks 50 yards apart.
5. Age 15 minutes.
6. Lay both tracks in a row.

Handler:

1. Keep dog on track on all legs.
2. Let dog up to 15' past corner.
3. Let dog investigate corner area.
4. When dog investigates next leg,
   lower tension to encourage.
5. As dog moves out on next leg,
   increase tension before you move
   off the corner.

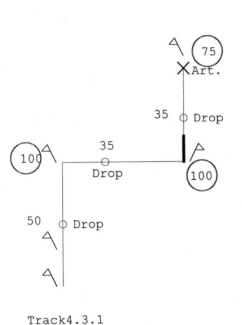

Track4.3.1

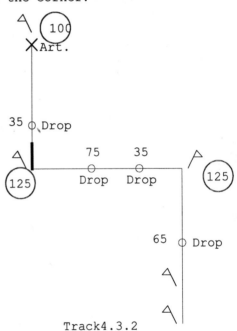

Track4.3.2

Purpose:
o   See session 4.1.

Tracklayer:
•   Short hard steps only the first 20 paces of the third leg.
o   See session 4.1.

Handler:
•   Practice Corner Communication Process.
o   See session 4.2.

Evaluation:
o   See session 4.1

Session 4.4

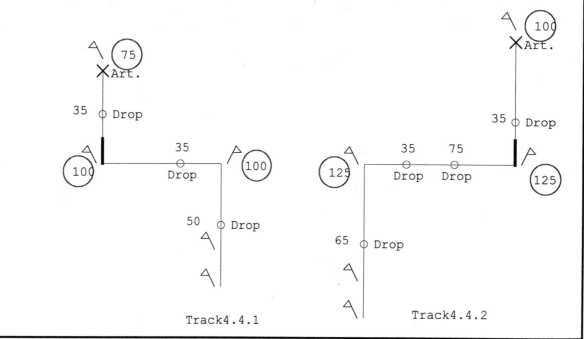

```
Tracklayer                          Handler:

1. Disregard wind unless dog        1. Keep dog on track on all legs.
   is having problems.              2. Let dog up to 15' past corner.
2. Short Hard Step first 20 yds     3. Let dog investigate corner area.
   of third leg.                    4. When dog investigates next leg,
3. Normal pace on first two legs.      lower tension to encourage.
4. Keep tracks 50 yards apart.      5. As dog moves out on next leg,
5. Age 15 minutes.                     increase tension before you move
6. Lay both tracks in a row.           off the corner.
```

Track4.4.1

Track4.4.2

Purpose:

o   See session 4.1.

Tracklayer:

o   See session 4.3.

Handler:

•   Practice Corner Communication Process.

o   See session 4.2.

Evaluation:

o   See session 4.1

Tracklayer

1. Disregard wind unless dog
   is having problems.
2. Normal pace on all legs.
3. Keep tracks 50 yards apart.
4. Age 15 minutes.
5. Lay both tracks in a row.

Handler:

1. Keep dog on track on all legs.
2. Let dog up to 15' past corner.
3. Let dog investigate corner area.
4. When dog investigates next leg,
   lower tension to encourage.
5. As dog moves out on next leg,
   increase tension before you move
   off the corner.

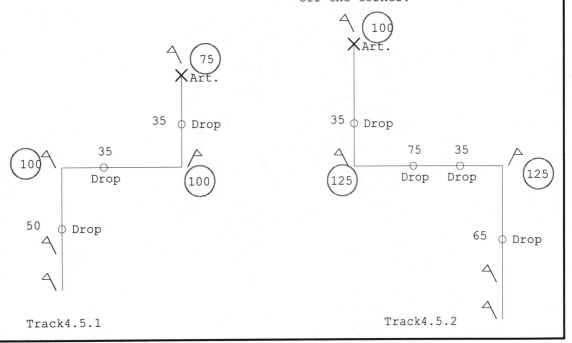

Track4.5.1   Track4.5.2

Purpose:

o   See session 4.1.

Tracklayer:

•   Normal steps on whole track.

o   See session 4.1.

Handler:

•   Practice Corner Communication Process.

o   See session 4.1.

Evaluation:

o   See session 4.1.

Tracklayer

1. Disregard wind unless dog is having problems.
2. Normal pace on all legs.
3. Keep tracks 50 yards apart.
4. Age 15 minutes.
5. Lay both tracks in a row.

Handler:

1. Keep dog on track on all legs.
2. Let dog up to 15' past corner.
3. Let dog investigate corner area.
4. When dog investigates next leg, lower tension to encourage.
5. As dog moves out on next leg, increase tension before you move off the corner.

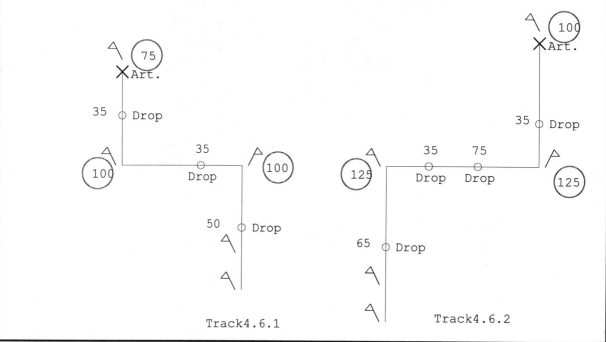

Track4.6.1   Track4.6.2

Purpose:
o   See session 4.1.

Tracklayer:
o   See session 4.5.

Handler:
•   Practice Corner Communication Process.
o   See session 4.2.

Evaluation:
o   See session 4.1.

Session 4.7

Purpose:
- Review the dog's progress and summarize his accomplishments.

Evaluation:
- You should be beginning to feel comfortable with your lead handling at the corners.
- Your dog should be enthusiastically tracking the legs and taking the corners with little problem.
- Write a summary of how your dog takes corners, how you handle him at the corners, and how to read him when he is past a corner and when he has taken the second leg.
- Write a review of his enthusiasm to start, his enthusiasm during the track, his enthusiasm on the corners, how close to the track he stays, how he reacts to the corners, and how he indicates the articles.
- Write down what you can do to encourage him to do better.

Phase 5. Reading the Dog.

Purpose:

- Teach handler to read dog without stakes.
- Teach dog to circle at the corners.
- Teach handler to organize search at corners.
- Age tracks to 25 minutes.

Strategy:

- Remove all but the first two stakes.
- Tracklayer must make a map.
- Tracklayer must leave haystacks at corners (except at acute corners).
- Use acute angle on a downhill, downwind leg to induce dog to overshoot corner and have to circle to find new leg.
- At least one of the acute angle tracks must be laid by someone other than the handler. Preferably, it should be the first such track (5.2).
- No haystack on the acute corner. We do not want anything to stop the dog at the corner.
- Design of tracks with acute angles is important. Layout must keep the scent of other legs from interfering with dog while on the acute. See suggested designs below.
- The tracklayer must know the exact location of the acute angle corner (to the footprint) and the exact direction of the next leg. The tracklayer may have to help a confused handler get his dog back on track.

Schedule:

Session	Track 1 Leg 1	Corner Angle	Track 1 Leg 2	Corner Angle	Track 1 Leg 3	Corner Angle	Track 1 Leg 4	Age	Total Length
5.1	100	90°	75	90°	100	90°	50	15	325
5.2	100	90°	100	135°	75	**45°**	125	15	400
5.3	100	90°	100	90°	125	90°	75	20	400
5.4	100	90°	100	**45°**	100	135°	150	20	450
5.5	125	90°	125	90°	125	90°	125	25	500
5.6	100	135°	150	90°	100	**45°**	150	25	500
5.7	Review								

Discussion:

Track 5.2 is the most exciting track of your short tracking career. It is your first real test - can you read your dog and can you organize your dog's search for a lost track. Those who know that the rules prohibit acute angle turns in test tracks may feel that this is an unfair test for an inexperienced dog and handler. As you will see in the discussion below, the point is to teach the handler and dog how to handle difficult corners, not to trick the dog. Nevertheless, fair or unfair, the test is a thrilling learning experience for the dogs and handlers who pass the test easily, for those who have to work at it, and even for those who need help from the tracklayer. What is really important to your future success as a tracking team is to learn from the test!

The tracks of the previous two phases were designed to teach the dog to notice the corner immediately and to take the new leg quickly and efficiently. By this stage, most dogs are noticing most corners within a few feet of the corner and are picking up the new leg with little delay. In addition, many dogs are marching around at least some of the corners without hesitation. This is great! It is exactly what we want our dogs to do. However, in a blind track, such as a certification or test track, the dog might have difficulty with a corner because of unusual tracking conditions. Because he might get some distance from a track, we must teach him how to find a new leg if he gets well past a corner or off a leg.

Downwind, downhill acute angle corners are used to induce the dog and handler to go past the corner. The wind blows the scent of the track past the corner giving the dog something to smell there. On a downhill leg, most dogs speed up, so they will naturally tend to overshoot the corner due to speed and momentum. Also, scent often drifts downhill, helping the wind carry the scent past the corner.

Should the track design work as planned, the dog will take the handler (who is 20' behind the dog) well past the corner. The tracklayer should stop the handler when the handler is 10' past the corner. So when the handler stops, the dog will have to circle behind the handler at least 10' to find the new leg.

The handler typically passes the corner and does not know where the next leg goes. The handler is going to feel quite lost. Nevertheless, it is important that the handler execute his job with care and confidence. His job, of course, is to organize the search, making sure the dog investigates all directions at several different distances from the handler.

As the handler follows on each new leg, notice a landmark overtop the dog. This is the handler's reference direction. In general, the track may go in any direction except straight back the way you have come. The corner may be anywhere else in front or behind the handler. The handler should also notice a groundmark at the stopping point so the handler can stay in place while pivoting.

The dog should circle the handler at various distances until he detects and takes the new leg. However, some dogs have learned in the last two phases of training that the corner is always between him and the handler. Therefore, the dog has had no reason to go behind the handler. These dogs will circle and search in front of the handler, but are reluctant to circle behind the handler. Such dogs will respond well to the pivoting described below.

The handler stops, continues to face the reference direction and expects the dog to search in front. If the dog circles in one direction or the other to about 60°, the handler should quietly pivot in that direction by 90°. The handler's reference direction should now be over one shoulder and the inward leg (and tracklayer) should be over the other shoulder. With luck, the dog will continue to search in that direction. When the dog again gets to 60° relative to the handler's new direction, the handler should again quietly pivot 90° to face directly back toward the inward leg and the tracklayer. Should the dog turn around and head back toward the reference direction, the handler should quite happily wait until the dog gets to 60° relative to the handler's direction and the pivot in that direction by 90°. So the Golden Search Rule is: *"**Whenever the dog gets within 30° of a shoulder, pivot toward that shoulder**"*.

At some point in this search, the dog will find the new leg and you will be off again. You will need to recognize his tracking behavior and be willing to go with the dog when he indicates the new leg. First, we need to discuss everything that can happen during an extensive search.

The handler controls the distance the dog circles from the handler. You want to get the dog to do two or three complete circles, each at a difference distance. The exact distances depend on the handler and the dog, but ideally, the first would be between 6' and 10', the second should be between 10' and 20', and the third would be between 20' and 40'. For an energetic dog, a third circle at 30' and a fourth circle at 40' is safer than a single third circle somewhere between 20' and 40'.

As the dog circles, you are noting and remembering exactly where he has searched and where he has not searched. One way to remember where he has searched is to keep a mental picture of a circle in mind and fill in the sections of the circle as the dog searches. The figure at the right shows a typical mental picture

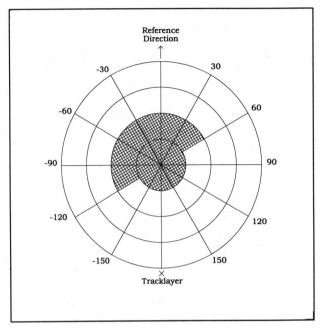

when the dog has completed one complete circle at 10 feet and has circled part of the next circle at 20 feet. If the dog has not committed to a new leg and there is an area he has not searched, you should pivot toward that direction until the dog searches it.

Once the dog has circled three or four times from this pivot point, the handler must be willing to back up about 15' toward the inward leg and try circling again. In a real test, the handler must be willing to back up several times. In this training exercise, once should be enough. Induce the dog to circle again at two or three distances. The dog will cross the new leg at several different places and at several different angles, so is likely to recognize it and commit to it on one of these crossing.

In all this circling, the dog will cross the inward leg several times. He may try to backtrack it. If he does, only let him go a few feet before increasing the tension and saying something like "Isn't that where we came from. Find the **good** track. **That's right**. **You** can find it." Steadily increase the tension until you have stopped the dog within 10' of his starting to backtrack or until he has diverged from the inward leg. Since we never double or triple lay any legs, he will quickly learn that there is nothing to be gained by backtracking.

If the dog comes to your feet and looks at you plaintively, he may be saying "I'm confused, help me". The first time he does this, encourage him to get back to tracking in a happy voice. If he does it repeatedly on a particular corner, or if he cannot be induced into searching again, it is time for you to move. Take a few steps back towards the inward leg. Happily, enthusiastically, excitedly, tell him something like: "**Find** it. Go ahead, **you** can find it. **Yes, you** can do it. That's **good, find** it!" Keep chatting to the dog, and keep taking steps backwards until you are to the corner (the tracklayer can tell you when you are at the corner). If the dog still won't search, take a few steps down the new leg and happily encourage the dog to "**Find** it!" Keep walking down the new leg with the dog on a short lead encouraging the dog to find it until the dog starts tracking again.

It is not a serious problem for the dog to quit on a complex new situation like this acute corner. By happily getting him past it, we teach him that there is more to find and that it fun to find it. The dog may feel it is unfair to be faced with something new and difficult, but we know that such situations are a necessary part of training. It is an important lesson for the dog to learn that even if he loses the track, he can find it again by diligently searching.

A dog that quits every time it is faced with a new situation or that repeatedly quits when faced with a difficult situation needs confidence building and tracking drive building. See the chapter on problem solving for some ideas. However, dogs that are taught using positive methods (like this one) are unlikely to develop serious quitting problems.

To recapitulate corner handling procedure:
- Stay 20' behind the dog as you approach the corner.
- Note a distant landmark in front of the dog.
- Allow the dog to take you past the corner, but no more than 10' past the corner.
- Note a landmark on the ground at your feet where you stop.
- Encourage the dog to circle.
- Turn 90° whenever the dog gets within 30° of either shoulder.
- Turn even earlier if the dog is stuck in one area and has not searched other areas.
- Control the distance the dog circles and have him circle at several distances.
- Back up to the corner if dog has circled three or four time or if he wants to quit.
- Encourage dog down the new leg if the dog won't take it.
- Stay calm and happy no matter how flustered you really want to be.

Tracklayer's Instructions

The tracklayer should realize it is important to know the exact location of the corner and the exact direction of the new leg. While laying the track, the tracklayer should make small haystacks at all corners except the acute. Make a haystack by twisting the grass into a tight stack and wrapping it round with a band of grass, or use surveyors tape, or orange clothespins. At the acute, note a landmark on the ground near the corner so it can be found later.

The tracklayer must make a map of the track as it is being laid. The map will help the tracklayer remember where the corners are and should be given to the handler after the track is run for the handler's journal.

For each leg, the tracklayer should note one or two distant landmarks in the direction of the new leg. It is much easier to walk in a straight line if you walk toward two distant landmarks. Show these landmarks on your map. Also note a nearby ground mark at each corner (haystack, tape, clothespin, rock, stick, flower).

While the track is being run, the tracklayer should:
- follow along behind the handler, but stop at least 10' before the corner.
- tell the handler to stop if he or she gets 10' past the corner.
- tell the handler where the corner is if the dog quits.
- tell the handler where the new leg goes if the dog quits.
- if the tracklayer is lost, admit it to the handler. The handler can decide whether to search for the track or just throw out a spare glove and play with the dog. The second course of action is usually the wisest.

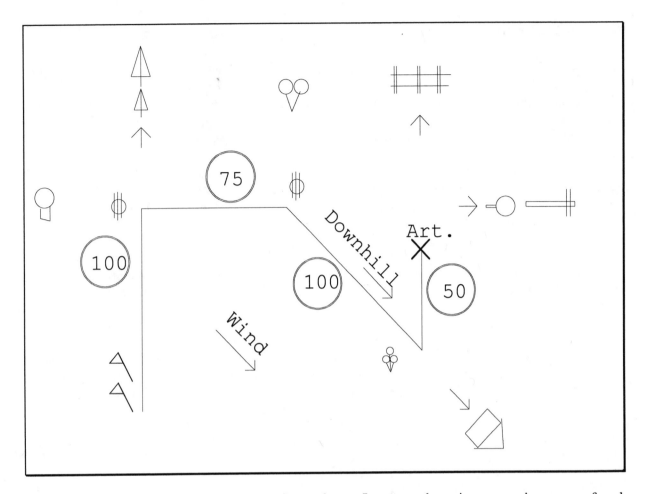

A typical field map looks something like the figure above. It may not be quite as neat since most of us do not yet have computers in the field. What is important about a map is to document the landmarks for each leg and each corner so you can exactly pinpoint the footsteps anywhere along the track that the dog gets in trouble. Map making skills take practice, but they are skills that will greatly enhance your own, your dog's, and your companion's dog's success in tracking.

How you lay the acute angle corner is important. At most corners, you stop at the corner while making a haystack, deciding what direction to go, and updating your map. At the acute, do not make the haystack, but do decide the next direction to go and update your map. However, at the acute, it is important that you stay facing the direction of the previous leg until you are ready to turn and step out in the new direction. Although you emit scent in all directions, many people believe that you emit more scent directly in front of you than to either side. So it is best to emit this extra scent in the direction we want the dog to overshoot the corner.

The location of the food drops leading into and out of the acute are important. We have two drops on the inward leg to speed the dog up. The second drop cannot be too close to the acute corner since a dog who stops at the drop may not pick up enough momentum to be carried past the corner. The drop coming out of the acute is an important reward for accomplishing a complex task. However, it cannot be too close to the corner or it will attract the dog onto the leg before he has a chance to overshoot the corner. Therefore, the drops should be 40 yards from the acute corner.

Reading Your Dog

Up until now, the handler has enjoyed well-marked tracks since the primary purpose was to teach the dog tracking skills. In the previous phase, you started to notice how your dog looked when he was tracking, how he looked when he veered off the track, how he looked when he overshot a corner, how he looked when he was searching for the new leg, how he committed to the new leg, and how he indicated the article. I hope that you paid careful attention, because now you will be quizzed.

Your skill in reading your dog was not perfected in the past twelve tracks, and will not be perfected in the next six. Your reading skills will continue to improve as you practice in varied conditions. You will continue to perfect your ability to read your dog as long as you track him. You must always strive to improve and refine these reading skills:

What is your dog's:
- body posture
- head carriage
- nose activity
- consistency of direction
- speed

when the dog is situated:
- on the track
- slightly off the track
- somewhat off the track
- well off the track
- approaching a corner
- on a corner
- past a corner
- way past a corner
- approaching a food drop
- near a food drop
- on an animal track
- near ground animals
- approaching an article
- near an article
- indicating an article

under various conditions:
- wind direction
- track age
- humidity
- time of day
- weather
- tracklayer individual
- tracklayer's footwear
- tracklayer's familiarity to the dog.

As you learn to read your dog in various situations and under various conditions, you will become more than a big bump at the end of the tracking line. You can know when to help the dog during training and you can supervise his tracking activity at his test.

At both your certification test and your TD test, you cannot help or guide your dog. However, if you can read your dog, you can avoid following him when he is obviously making a mistake. As an extreme example, you might be happily tracking along when your dog notices a couple picnicking off to the side of the track. Say the dog turns toward the picnickers. Is he dashing over to them to beg for food or is he taking a corner? You should be able to read your dog well enough to know the difference. Most judges will accept your stopping your dog from going to the picnickers if they think you can tell whether the dog is tracking or not. Luckily, most judges are experienced at reading dogs so they can read the same things in your dog as you can.

```
Tracklayer:                          Handler:

1. Choose and lay only one           1. Try to get someone else to lay
   of alternative tracks shown.         at least one normal track and
   OK to flip all corners, e.g.         one "acute" track this phase.
   from Right-Right-Left to          2. Don't watch track being laid
   Left-Left-Right.                  3. Read your dog.
2. Normal pace on all legs.          4. Note landmarks on each leg.
3. Make a map, show landmarks.       5. Discuss what happened with
4. Make haystacks.                      tracklayer after the track.
5. Age 15 minutes.
```

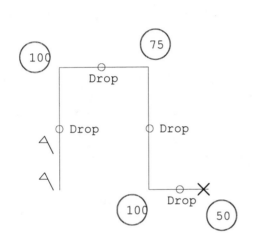

Track 5.1 (Alternative A)

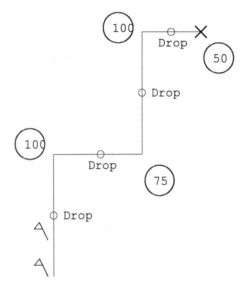

Track 5.1 (Alternative B)

Purpose:
- Introduce three turn tracks and practice reading the dog.

Tracklayer:
- Make a map of these tracks as you lay them and include landmarks.
- Extend your arms at the corners to sight landmarks at 90 degrees.
- Use only two flags at start and 30 yards.
- Use haystacks or natural ground markers for corners.

Handler:
- If someone else (reliable) can lay the track, don't watch the track being laid.
- Learn to read your dog - on track, off track, at a corner, on a new leg.
- Note landmarks for each leg.

Evaluation:
- Note how dog works the corners and how he maintains his attitude on each leg.
- Note how you are reading your dog - what signs indicate he is on or off the track.

Session 5.2

```
Tracklayer:                          Handler:

1. Choose and lay only one           1. Try to get someone else to lay
   of alternative tracks shown.         at least one normal track and
   OK to flip all corners, e.g.         one "acute"  track this phase.
   from Right-Right-Left to          2. Don't watch track being laid
   Left-Left-Right.                  3. Read your dog.
2. Normal pace on all legs.          4. Note landmarks on each leg.
3. Make a map, show landmarks.       5. Discuss what happened with
4. Make haystacks except at acute.      tracklayer after the track.
5. Age 15 minutes.
```

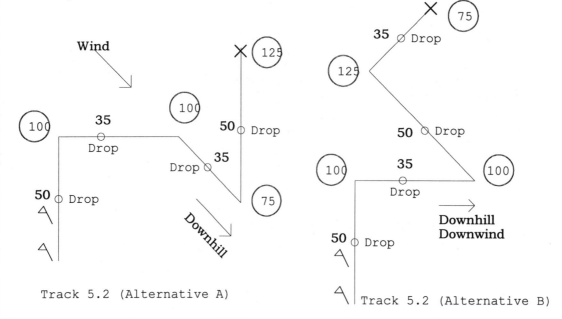

Track 5.2 (Alternative A)   Track 5.2 (Alternative B)

Purpose:
- Teach dog to circle behind handler when a corner is overshot.
- See session 5.1.

Tracklayer:
- See session 5.1.

Handler:
- Work on reading your dog.
- Work on handling dog at corners.
- See session 5.1

Evaluation:
- Note how dog handled acute angle turn.
- See session 5.1

Tracklayer:

1. Choose and lay only one
   of alternative tracks shown.
   OK to flip all corners, e.g.
   from Left-Left-Right to
   Right-Right-Left.
2. Normal pace on all legs.
3. Make a map, show landmarks.
4. Make haystacks.
5. Age 15 minutes.

Handler:

1. Try to get someone else to lay
   at least one normal track and
   one "acute" track this phase.
2. Don't watch track being laid
3. Read your dog.
4. Note landmarks on each leg.
5. Discuss what happened with
   tracklayer after the track.

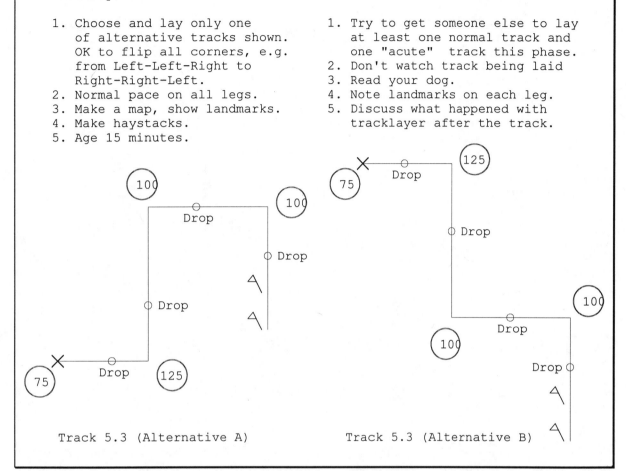

Track 5.3 (Alternative A)   Track 5.3 (Alternative B)

Purpose:
o   See session 5.1.

Tracklayer:
o   See session 5.1.

Handler:
o   See session 5.1.

Evaluation:
o   See session 5.1.

Session 5.4

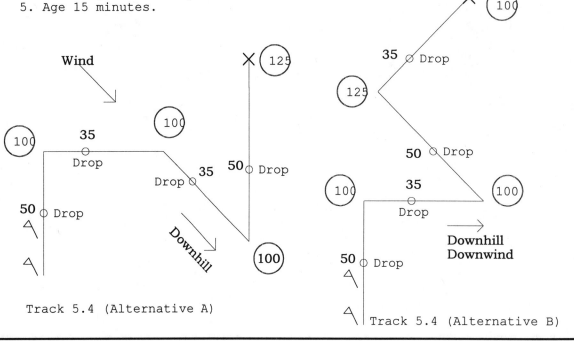

Tracklayer:

1. Choose and lay only one of alternative tracks shown. OK to flip all corners, e.g. from Right-Right-Left to Left-Left-Right.
2. Normal pace on all legs.
3. Make a map, show landmarks.
4. Make haystacks except at acute.
5. Age 15 minutes.

Handler:

1. Try to get someone else to lay at least one normal track and one "acute" track this phase.
2. Don't watch track being laid
3. Read your dog.
4. Note landmarks on each leg.
5. Discuss.

Track 5.4 (Alternative A)

Track 5.4 (Alternative B)

Purpose:

o   See session 5.2.

Tracklayer:

o   See session 5.2.

Handler:

o   See session 5.2.

Evaluation:

o   See session 5.2.

Tracklayer:

1. Choose and lay only one
   of alternative tracks shown.
   OK to flip all corners, e.g.
   from Left-Right-Right to
   Right-Left-Left.
2. Normal pace on all legs.
3. Make a map, show landmarks.
4. Make haystacks.
5. Age 15 minutes.

Handler:

1. Try to get someone else to lay
   at least one normal track and
   one "acute" track this phase.
2. Don't watch track being laid
3. Read your dog.
4. Note landmarks on each leg.
5. Discuss what happened with
   tracklayer after the track.

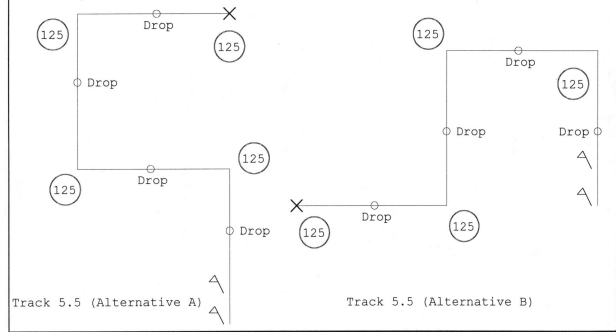

Track 5.5 (Alternative A)

Track 5.5 (Alternative B)

Purpose:

o   See session 5.1.

Tracklayer:

o   See session 5.1.

Handler:

o   See session 5.1.

Evaluation:

o   See session 5.1.

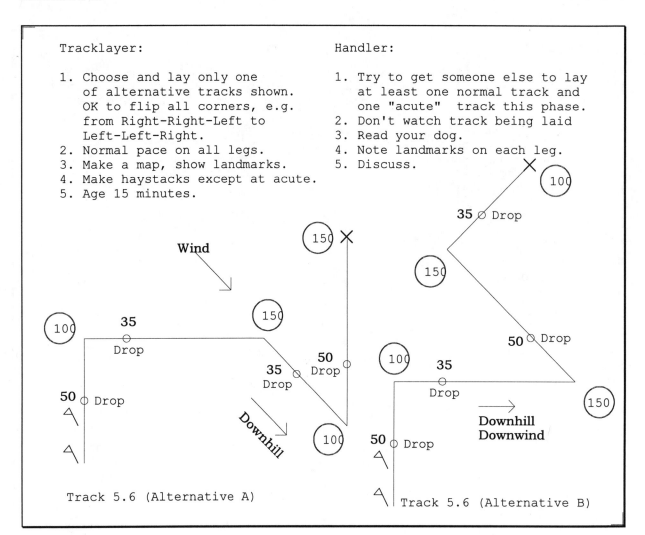

Tracklayer:

1. Choose and lay only one
   of alternative tracks shown.
   OK to flip all corners, e.g.
   from Right-Right-Left to
   Left-Left-Right.
2. Normal pace on all legs.
3. Make a map, show landmarks.
4. Make haystacks except at acute.
5. Age 15 minutes.

Handler:

1. Try to get someone else to lay
   at least one normal track and
   one "acute" track this phase.
2. Don't watch track being laid
3. Read your dog.
4. Note landmarks on each leg.
5. Discuss.

Track 5.6 (Alternative A)

Track 5.6 (Alternative B)

Purpose:
o   See session 5.2.

Tracklayer:
o   See session 5.2.

Handler:
o   See session 5.2.

Evaluation:
o   See session 5.2.

Session 5.7

Purpose:
- Review the dog's progress and summarize his accomplishments.

Evaluation:

- You should be beginning to feel comfortable reading your dog on straight legs and at corners.
- Your dog should be comfortable finding the new leg at corners, even if some searching is required.
- Some slight drop in the efficiency of taking corners is often a consequence of the dog realizing that there are more possibilities than tracks that just go straight ahead and tracks that just turn squarely right or left. Compare your dog's handling of 90° corners at the end of phase 4 with his handling of 90° corners now.
- Write a summary of how your dog takes acute corners, how you handle him when he has to search for the track, and how to read him when he is past a corner and when he has taken the new leg.

Summary:

By accomplishing these six tracks, you have passed the most significant milestones in tracking -- you are beginning to read your dog and your dog is beginning to understand that he can circle and find the track when it is lost.

Unless your dog is experiencing motivational problems, you and the dog have a fair chance of passing a certification test now. Nevertheless, there are additional skills you both need to perfect. Therefore, unless you are in a very big rush, it is wisest to wait until your dog is experienced with both 45-minute-old tracks and complex tracks before asking to be certified.

If your dog is experiencing motivational problems, you must determine what you have done to cause this lack of motivation or what you failed to do to properly encourage motivational tracking drive. Look at your journal and see when was the last time he was consistently motivated. Consider the following common possibilities:
- Did you progress too fast for the dog shortly before you noticed this drop in motivation?
- Did the weather get hot recently?
- Have you allowed the tracks to get older than 15 minutes?
- Have you reduced your own show of enthusiasm for his tracking accomplishments?

Many dogs are more sensitive to us than we think they are. Most dogs read their handlers better than handlers read their dogs. In general, you want to go back to where the dog was last motivated and redo the material again. Perhaps you need to progress more slowly, use shorter tracks, have more food on the track, or play longer after the track is completed. Whatever you do, make some changes. Continuing with the program from here with an unmotivated dog is unlikely to lead to tracking success. Look ahead at Chapter 7 for a further discussion of motivation.

Phase 6. Track Age.

Purpose:

- Teach dog to happily track 30 to 50 minute old tracks.
- Make dog thoroughly familiar and happy with TD complexity tracks.
- Practice reading the dog.

Strategy Overview:

- Alternate sessions between track age and reading the dog to help maintain dog's motivation.
- Track-age sessions use two tracks, a younger one and an older one.
- Carefully observe dog's enthusiasm to track.

Schedule Overview:

Session	Track 1 Legs	Track 1 Turns	Track 1 Length	Track 1 Age	Track 2 Legs	Track 2 Turns	Track 2 Length	Age	Total Length
6.1	3	Right	250	20	3	Left	250	30	500
6.2	4-5	R & L	400-500	25					400-500
6.3	3	Left	250	25	3	Right	250	35	500
6.4	4-5	R & L	400-500	25					400-500
6.5	3	Right	300	30	3	Left	300	40	600
6.6	4-5	R & L	400-500	30					400-500
6.7	3	Left	300	35	3	Right	300	45	600
6.8	4-5	R & L	400-500	30					400-500
6.9	3	Right	300	40	3	Left	300	50	600
6.10	4-5	R & L	400-500	30					400-500
6.11	Review								

Discussion:

It is time for the dog to learn to follow older tracks. Up until now, your dog has followed tracks up to 25 minutes old. We want him to happily follow tracks up to 50 minutes old. A TD test track is 30 minutes to 2 hours old, but the vast majority of them are 30 to 50 minutes old. Therefore, we want to concentrate on getting the dog to be a happy tracker in this time range

We don't immediately try to get them to track 1-2 hour old tracks since 1) many dogs will face motivational problems if introduced to older tracks too quickly and 2) dogs who can track 2-hour-old tracks typically also notice 24-hour-old tracks. There is considerable proofing required to teach a dog to stay with the 2 hour old track rather than be attracted off on the 24 hour old track. Due to the way test tracks are laid out the day before the test, 24-hour-old conflicting tracks are common at a test. Unless you have trouble getting into a test and have lots of time to train, your best odds for passing a TD test are to train an enthusiastic 30-50 minute old tracker rather than confuse the dog with age related problems.

We introduce age in a carefully controlled fashion because of the phenomenon Glen Johnson called the "Hump". Your dog has been following some combination of person scent and ground scent - both have been in generous supply and have been easy for the dog to follow. As you remember from the introductory chapter, the personal scent is from the particles that have fallen off the tracklayer and the ground scent is from the vegetation crushed and dirt disturbed by the tracklayer's footsteps. As we age the tracks, the personal scent seems to dissipate more rapidly than the ground scent. So at some point, the predominate scent changes from personal scent to ground scent. When this happens, most dogs show loss of track and act as if they can't smell any track. The timing when the "Hump" occurs varies primarily with temperature and humidity; it is also influenced by all the other factors that affect scenting: wind, weather, sunlight, rain, ground cover, dirt compactness, tracklayer, and the dog.

When the dog faces the "Hump" and quits, we want to be in a situation where we can help the dog. We will gently and positively lead the dog through the track until he picks it up. Through this process, the dog will realize that this ground scent alone leads to the hotdogs and the glove, and is just as fun to track as the combined person scent and ground scent.

The technique is to lay well-marked simple U-shaped tracks so we know where the track goes if and when the dog quits. We lay two of these tracks per session, and run the fresher track first to motivate the dog on the first fresh track. That's right, lay the two tracks in one order and run them in the opposite order. You will need to lay the tracks quickly and efficiently and be ready to run the dog as soon as the second one ages sufficiently.

According to theory, the hump is most likely to occur on the older of the two tracks. However, wind, weather, and temperature are difficult things to theorize about accurately, so the hump may occur on the first track as well. We use flags on both tracks so we will be able to confidently lead our dogs through the hump whenever it happens.

Every other session, train TD complexity tracks to give the dog experience with these types of tracks and to give the owner additional practice in reading their dog in a variety of conditions. One important reason we alternate the age sessions and the 4-5 leg sessions is to avoid burnout while aging the tracks. Some handlers get bored laying five straight sessions of two U-shaped tracks when they are sure their dog is ready for TD complexity tracks and that they need more practice reading their dog. In fact, many of the U-shaped tracks are uneventful. Nevertheless, they should be fun for the dog and it is up to the handler to assure that fun. On the other hand, dogs that are forced to learn age too quickly seem to lose enthusiasm. So the alternating schedule is designed to allow the dog to unstressfully learn age without losing motivation while giving the dog and handler additional practice to improve skills taught in previous phases.

Look ahead to when the tracking tests are held in your area. For AKC tests, your dog will need to be certified by a tracking judge that he is ready to enter tests before you can enter. The judge does so by giving you a test track. You will need to have the AKC Tracking Regulations and be familiar with the rules.

Some dogs and handlers are ready to enter tests at the conclusion of this phase. Some dogs may need more practice with different tracking conditions, additional work to clarify issues, or more fun to raise their level of enthusiasm. Some handlers may need more work reading their dog. Most dogs and handlers who follow this training method will be ready by the end of this phase. If you feel you and your dog are ready, contact a judge in your area to arrange for the certification.

Tracklayer:

1. Lay 6.1.2 first, then 6.1.1.
2. Normal pace on all legs.
3. Make a map, show landmarks.
4. Use Stakes at corners.
5. Age 6.1.1 20 minutes
   and 6.1.2 30 minutes.

Handler:

1. Try to run dog on schedule.
2. If dog quits, take thru track
   using a happy tone of voice
   until dog picks up again.
3. Read your dog.

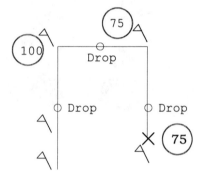

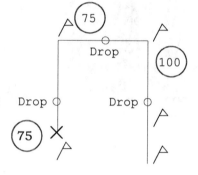

Track 6.1.1
Lay this track second!

Track 6.1.2
Lay this track first!

Purpose:
* Age tracks and get over the "hump".

Tracklayer:
* Use flags at the start, 30 yards, on all the corners, and after the article.
* The handler must know where the track is so the dog can helped if needed.

Handler:
* These are good tracks to lay yourself.
* If your dog quits, just happily lead your dog through the rest of the track.

Evaluation:
* Note how dog works the tracks as they get older.

Session 6.2

Tracklayer:

1. Design a TD style track
   with 4-5 turns,
   use both right and left turns,
   total length 400-500 yards.
2. Normal pace on all legs.
3. Make a map, show landmarks.
4. Use haystacks or ground
   markers at each corner.
5. Age 25 minutes.

Handler:

1. Try to run dog on schedule.
2. If dog quits, take thru track
   using a happy tone of voice
   until dog picks up again.
3. Read your dog.

Track 6.2
Example A
400 yards

Track 6.2
Example B
420 yards

Purpose:
- Practice reading your dog.
- Build perseverance when food is not present by moving drops toward middle or end of track.

Tracklayer:
- Mark all corners and after the article with a haystack or ground marker.
- You must know where the track is so you can help the handler if the dog gets lost.

Handler:
- These are good tracks to lay yourself. Keep your eyes on the dog until he commits to a new leg, then look up and confirm that he is going in the correct direction. A hat with a large bill or brim can help you avoid inadvertently looking ahead on the track.
- Work on your corner handling and communicating with your dog.
- If your dog quits, just happily lead your dog through the rest of the track.

Evaluation:
- Note how dog works the corners.

```
Tracklayer:                          Handler:

1. Lay 6.3.2 first, then 6.3.1.      1. Try to run dog on schedule.
2. Normal pace on all legs.          2. If dog quits, take thru track
3. Make a map, show landmarks.          using a happy tone of voice
4. Use Stakes at corners.               until dog picks up again.
5. Age 6.3.1 25 minutes              3. Read your dog.
   and 6.3.2 35 minutes.
```

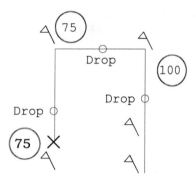

Track 6.3.1
Lay this track second!

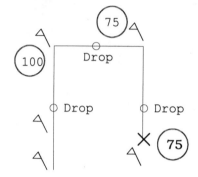

Track 6.3.2
Lay this track first!

Purpose:
- Age tracks and get over the "hump".

Tracklayer:
- Use flags at the start, 30 yards, all corners, and after the article.
- The handler must know where the track is so the dog can be helped if needed.

Handler:
- These are good tracks to lay yourself.
- If your dog quits, just happily lead your dog through the rest of the track.

Evaluation:
- Note how dog works the tracks as they get older.

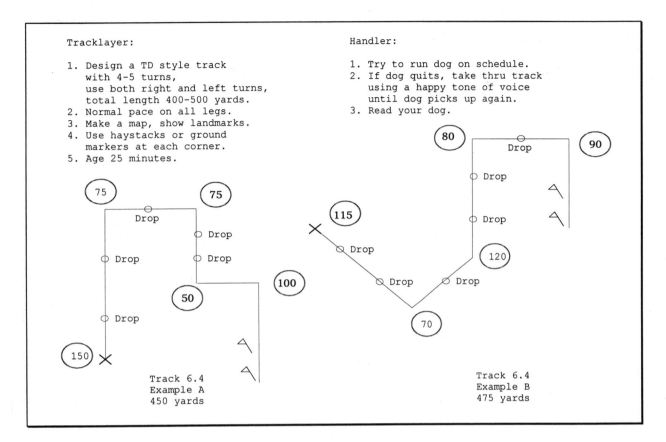

Tracklayer:

1. Design a TD style track
   with 4-5 turns,
   use both right and left turns,
   total length 400-500 yards.
2. Normal pace on all legs.
3. Make a map, show landmarks.
4. Use haystacks or ground
   markers at each corner.
5. Age 25 minutes.

Handler:

1. Try to run dog on schedule.
2. If dog quits, take thru track
   using a happy tone of voice
   until dog picks up again.
3. Read your dog.

Track 6.4
Example A
450 yards

Track 6.4
Example B
475 yards

Purpose:
- Practice reading your dog.
- Build perseverance when food is not present by moving drops toward middle or end of track.

Tracklayer:
- Use flags at start, 30 yards.
- Mark all corners and after the article with a haystack or ground marker.
- You must know where the track is so you can help the handler if the dog gets lost.

Handler:
- These are good tracks to lay yourself. Keep your eyes on the dog until he commits to a new leg, then look up and confirm that he is going in the correct direction. A hat with a large bill or brim can help you avoid inadvertently looking ahead on the track.
- Work on your corner handling and communicating with your dog.
- If your dog quits, just happily lead your dog through the rest of the track.

Evaluation:
- Note how dog works the corners.

Tracklayer:

1. Lay 6.5.2 first, then 6.5.1.
2. Normal pace on all legs.
3. Make a map, show landmarks.
4. Use Stakes at corners.
5. Age 6.5.1 30 minutes
   and 6.5.2 40 minutes.

Handler:

1. Try to run dog on schedule.
2. If dog quits, take thru track
   using a happy tone of voice
   until dog picks up again.
3. Read your dog.

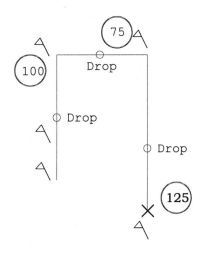

Track 6.5.1
Lay this track second!

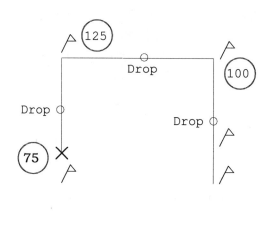

Track 6.5.2
Lay this track first!

Purpose:
- Age tracks and get over the "hump".

Tracklayer:
- Use flags at the start, 30 yards, all the corners, and after the article.
- The handler must know where the track is so the dog can be helped if needed.

Handler:
- These are good tracks to lay yourself.
- If your dog quits, just happily lead your dog through the rest of the track.

Evaluation:
- Note how dog works the tracks as they get older.

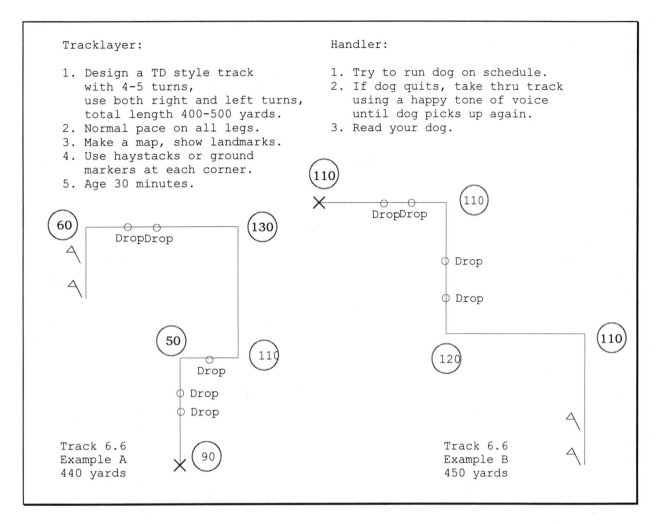

Tracklayer:

1. Design a TD style track
   with 4-5 turns,
   use both right and left turns,
   total length 400-500 yards.
2. Normal pace on all legs.
3. Make a map, show landmarks.
4. Use haystacks or ground
   markers at each corner.
5. Age 30 minutes.

Handler:

1. Try to run dog on schedule.
2. If dog quits, take thru track
   using a happy tone of voice
   until dog picks up again.
3. Read your dog.

Track 6.6
Example A
440 yards

Track 6.6
Example B
450 yards

Purpose:
- Practice reading your dog.
- Build perseverance when food is not present by moving drops toward middle or end of track.

Tracklayer:
- Use flags at start, 30 yards.
- Mark all corners and after the article with a haystack or ground marker.
- You must know where the track is so you can help the handler if the dog gets lost.

Handler:
- These are good tracks to lay yourself. Keep your eyes on the dog until he commits to a new leg, then look up and confirm that he is going in the correct direction. A hat with a large bill or brim can help you avoid inadvertently looking ahead on the track.
- Work on your corner handling and communicating with your dog.
- If your dog quits, just happily lead your dog through the rest of the track.

Evaluation:
- Note how dog works the corners.

```
Tracklayer:                        Handler:

1. Lay 6.7.2 first, then 6.7.1.    1. Try to run dog on schedule.
2. Normal pace on all legs.        2. If dog quits, take thru track
3. Make a map, show landmarks.        using a happy tone of voice
4. Use Stakes at corners.             until dog picks up again.
5. Age 6.7.1 35 minutes            3. Read your dog.
   and 6.7.2 45 minutes.
```

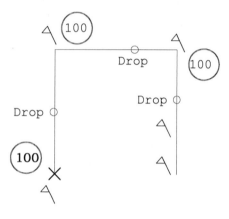

Track 6.7.1
Lay this track second!

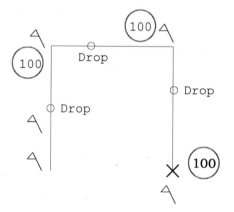

Track 6.7.2
Lay this track first!

Purpose:
*   Age tracks and get over the "hump".

Tracklayer:
*   Use flags at the start, 30 yards, all the corners, and after the article.
*   The handler must know where the track is so the dog can be helped if needed.

Handler:
*   These are good tracks to lay yourself.
*   If your dog quits, just happily lead your dog through the rest of the track.

Evaluation:
*   Note how dog works the tracks as they get older.

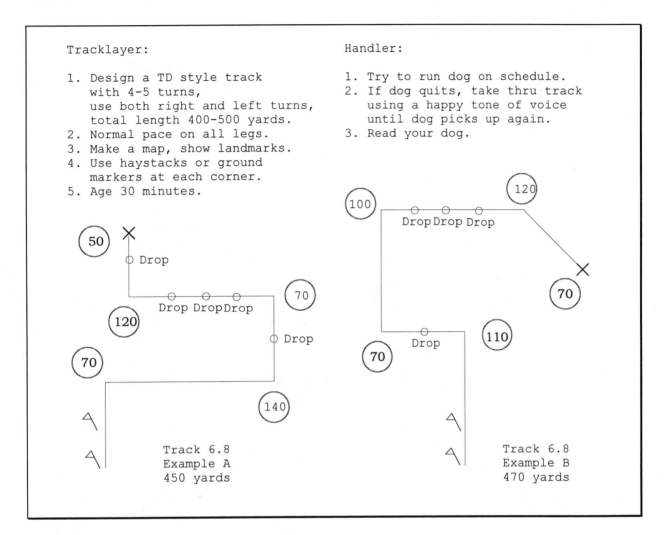

Tracklayer:

1. Design a TD style track
   with 4-5 turns,
   use both right and left turns,
   total length 400-500 yards.
2. Normal pace on all legs.
3. Make a map, show landmarks.
4. Use haystacks or ground
   markers at each corner.
5. Age 30 minutes.

Handler:

1. Try to run dog on schedule.
2. If dog quits, take thru track
   using a happy tone of voice
   until dog picks up again.
3. Read your dog.

Track 6.8
Example A
450 yards

Track 6.8
Example B
470 yards

Purpose:
- Build perseverance when food is not present by moving drops toward middle or end of track.

Tracklayer:
- Use flags at start, 30 yards.
- Mark all corners and after the article with a haystack or ground marker.
- You must know where the track is so you can help the handler if the dog gets lost.

Handler:
- These are good tracks to lay yourself. Keep your eyes on the dog until he commits to a new leg, then look up and confirm that he is going in the correct direction. A hat with a large bill or brim can help you avoid inadvertently looking ahead on the track.
- Work on your corner handling and communicating with your dog.
- If your dog quits, just happily lead your dog through the rest of the track.

Evaluation:
- Note how dog works the corners.

```
Tracklayer:                          Handler:

1. Lay 6.9.2 first, then 6.9.1.      1. Try to run dog on schedule.
2. Normal pace on all legs.          2. If dog quits, take thru track
3. Make a map, show landmarks.          using a happy tone of voice
4. Use Stakes at corners.               until dog picks up again.
5. Age 6.9.1 40 minutes              3. Read your dog.
   and 6.9.2 50 minutes.
```

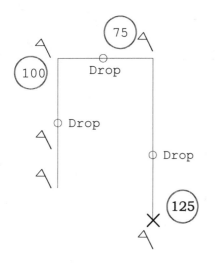

Track 6.9.1
Lay this track second!

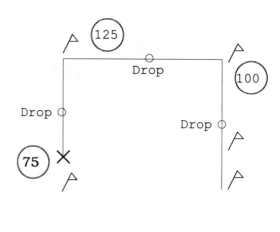

Track 6.9.2
Lay this track first!

Purpose:
- Age tracks and get over the "hump".

Tracklayer:
- Use flags at the start, 30 yards, all the corners, and after the article.
- The handler must know where the track is so the dog can be helped if needed.

Handler:
- These are good tracks to lay yourself.
- If your dog quits, just happily lead your dog through the rest of the track.

Evaluation:
- Note how dog works the tracks as they get older.

Tracklayer:

1. Design a TD style track
   with 4-5 turns,
   use both right and left turns,
   total length 400-500 yards.
2. Normal pace on all legs.
3. Make a map, show landmarks.
4. Use haystacks or ground
   markers at each corner.
5. Age 30 minutes.

Handler:

1. Try to run dog on schedule.
2. If dog quits, take thru track
   using a happy tone of voice
   until dog picks up again.
3. Read your dog.

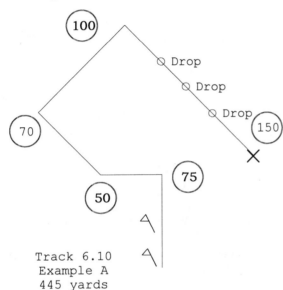

Track 6.10
Example A
445 yards

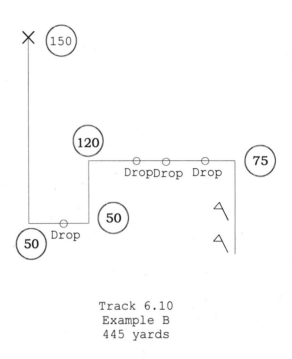

Track 6.10
Example B
445 yards

Purpose:
- Build perseverance when food is not present by moving drops toward middle or end of track.

Tracklayer:
- Use flags at start, 30 yards.
- Mark all corners and after the article with a haystack or ground marker.
- You must know where the track is so you can help the handler if the dog gets lost.

Handler:
- These are good tracks to lay yourself. Keep your eyes on the dog until he commits to a new leg, then look up and confirm that he is going in the correct direction. A hat with a large bill or brim can help you avoid inadvertently looking ahead on the track.
- Work on your corner handling and communicating with your dog.
- If your dog quits, just happily lead your dog through the rest of the track.

Evaluation:
- Note how dog works the corners.

Session 6.11 Review and Evaluation

Now is an excellent time to review your dog's tracking performance and your handling skills. In the next chapter, you will use this evaluation to individualize your training program to the needs of you and your dog. Your future tracking success will be enhanced by objectively evaluating you and your dog, so spend a few minutes now to think about these questions. If you have trouble being truly objective when it comes to your best canine companion, you may find it helpful to have a tracking friend help you do the evaluation. Consider their perspective, but you are responsible for the evaluation.

These questions should be answered based on your dog's performance in his last five TD-like tracks, if you have followed the schedule exactly, that is sessions 6.2, 6.4, 6.6, 6.8, and 6.10. If an unusual event occurred on one of these sessions (say a soccer team started to play right in the middle of your track), drop that session from your consideration and add session 5.6.

> When you arrive at the tracking field, is your dog obviously excited to be there and obviously impatient for his track?

> In the last five TD-like tracks, did you help him find the track more than once?

> On the best 80% of his opportunities to work a corner, does he find and commit to the new leg quickly and enthusiastically?

> On the best 80% of your opportunities to read your dog on a corner (without flags), do you read his tracking behavior and believe your dog quickly and confidently?

These questions may require a little amplification, so I will discuss what I look for in more detail.

For question 1, I am not interested in how the dog shows excitement. I am only interested in whether he anticipates the fun he is going to have as soon as he gets to the tracking field.

For question 2, I am very objective about what it means to help a dog. I don't count any normal training-handling techniques such as increasing the tension or raising my arm if the dog gets a little off the track. I do count places where I have to point out the track to him or keep him from committing to a false direction. The only exception to counting these places is if the dog was committing to an obvious distraction and he went back to tracking promptly when I asked him to "Find the good track".

For question 3, I am looking for the dog's behavior to be purposeful and easy to read the vast majority of the time. I would like 100% here, and certainly expect more than 90% before the dog actually gets to a test, but at this stage I am not concerned if it is a little less than that.

For question 4, I am looking for the handler's ability to read the dog the vast majority of the time. Experienced handlers should have 99% ratings, but it takes time to accumulate the experience needed to consistently to read your dog and the confidence to consistently believe him.

Phase 7. Perfecting Skills.

Purpose:

- Improve motivation, skill, commitment, and communication.
- Make dog thoroughly familiar and happy with TD complexity tracks.

Strategy:

- Customize the tracking work to address individual aspects of training that need improvement.
- Maintain and build enthusiasm.

Discussion:

If you have not yet done session 6.11 (evaluation) in the previous chapter, please do that now before proceeding. You will use the results of that evaluation to customize your training plan.

Following this process to evaluate your dog and prescribe a customized tracking plan suited to your dog is complicated. It is almost like having a private lesson with an expert. It requires such care in following detailed directions that some people may want to skip the whole thing. Since the full customization method will more accurately and finely describe a plan suited to you and your dog's training needs, I strongly encourage you to try to use the full method. There is a short-cut method shown on the next page for those who have too much difficulty completing this more complicated process.

In setting up the custom-tracking plan, each question is first considered individually, then a chart is used to select one of six training plans. The chosen training plan is further customized to match you and your dog's particular situation.

1. Ideally, your dog is having so much fun so consistently that it jumps around and barks excitedly as you drive up to your favorite tracking field. However, it is quite reasonable to answer yes to this question for any form of excitement the dog shows in this situation. The essential point is that the dog anticipates what is coming up as soon as he has a clue that he will soon get to track. If you answered yes to this question, continue your current level of motivational rewards for the dog.

    If your dog is excited and happy when he is actually tracking but fails to anticipate the fun when you arrive at the tracking site, you may question how extensively you need to increase his motivational drive to track. As you remember, I am not interested in how the dog shows excitement, just that he shows it some way. You probably don't have to increase your level of motivation a lot, but it would help if you increased it some. A laid-back dog that cannot bother to show excitement in anticipation of the track will be a better tracking dog if his motivational drive is increased.

    If your dog is not showing excitement, either on the track or as you arrive at the tracking site, you need to substantially increase the positive motivational rewards he gets for working for you. You have to discover what really motivates him. It may be food, or special food, or toys, or special toys, or a tennis ball, or getting to go for a big run, or a wild wrestling match with you, or something else. It does not matter what it is; it only matters that you provide it for your dog at the end of the track in a way that the dog values highly.

If a dog has regular access to a reward, he will value it less than if it is special. If your dog is even a tiny bit overweight, put him on a diet. Don't feed him for at least 12 hours before tracking unless he has a medical condition that requires more frequent feeding. Whether or not he is overweight, move most of his regular meal to the end of the track. If your dog has free access to toys at home, pick them up and only give him toys as a reward for tracking. By washing the toys after each use, you remove the old saliva and make the toy fresh and special again. Toys survive machine washing and drying many times. Even the ones that make electronic noises can be washed in a machine.

Remember to enjoy yourself and show your pride in your dog's accomplishment. It is a whole lot easier for the dog to be happy about tracking if you are happy about where you are, what you are doing, and what the dog is doing. Find something good in any situation and say something aloud to the dog about it. If you are a reserved person, get rambunctious and loud. If you are a talkative person, praise your dog softly. Your dog is doing something very special with you, show him your appreciation in a special way.

At this point, you have established your current evaluation of your dog into one of three categories:
   Anticipates: anticipates when you arrive at the tracking site the fun he will have tracking,
   On-track: has lots of fun on the track itself, but does not get excited until the track,
   Unexcited: does not get enthusiastic or excited on the track.

2.   As the discussion in session 6.11 emphasized, you need to be very objective when evaluating what it means to help your dog. In training, we freely help the dog whenever they need help (once we give them ample opportunity to solve the situation themselves). In a test, you are not going to know where the track goes and you are not going to be able to help your dog. Therefore, it is important to monitor how many times you need to help and use that information to fine-tune the level of difficulty of the tracks.

If the dog gets in trouble too often, say once or twice per track, he is likely to either get discouraged or expect help from you whenever he loses the track. So you need to back off on the difficulty of the tracks until he gains confidence and skill in the problems he must solve.

On the other hand, if he never needs any help, we must evaluate if he is facing difficult enough challenges. If the two of you are working blind TD test-like tracks in new locations, then you

---

Shortcut Plan.

Some readers may find this customization process too detailed and complicated. Although it is a valuable process to go through, those of you who really wish to *wing it* may want to take a shortcut here. The shortcut method requires you make a three way choice as follows:

If your dog needs additional motivation, do Plan F (page126), then go on to Phase 8.
If you or your dog need a little more work, do Plan C (page 118), then go on to Phase 8.
Otherwise, do Plan A (page 115), then go on to Phase 8.

I do recommend you go through the full customization plan. It will more finely tune your training to you and your dog's actual needs. Nevertheless, the shortcut method will work for many of you and is a better alternative than quitting.

---

need not increase the difficulty. If not, gradually increase the difficulty of the tracks until they more closely match the requirements of the test.

The third situation is where you need to help him less than once per track but more than once in the last five tracks. You are probably progressing nicely and so long as you see no signs of loss of motivation, you can keep up the same level of difficulty.

Therefore, you have now evaluated your dog into one of three categories:
0 – 1: one or less times helped in last five TD-like tracks.
2 – 4: two-to-four times helped in the last five TD-like tracks.
5 or more: five or more times helped in the last five TD-like tracks.

3.   Whether or not the dog needs help, he may be easy or hard to read. A dog that is easy to read is a joy to track. It is well worth the effort to structure your training to maximize the ease with which he can be read. Review the discussion on corners in chapters 3-5.

To be easy to read, the dog needs to follow the straight legs close to the track, show loss of track distinctively, search for the new leg purposefully, and commit to the new leg quickly and irresistibly.

Each aspect should be worked on separately. Focus on the first one listed above that has weakness and set up tracks to improve that aspect. Then augment your training plan to improve the remaining aspects until your dog is easy to read.

For a dog that is not following overtop the footsteps, put markers or flags every 50 yards and move up the line so you are only ten feet behind the dog. Use line tension, and use raising and lowering your arm to keep the dog close to the track. Narrow your definition of being close to the track. Use lots of food on the track to reward the dog for being close to the track.

For the dog that does not show a distinctive loss of track, use corner markers ten-feet before each corner and work ten-feet behind your dog. When you come alongside the flag, the dog is on the corner. Slow him up and stop him within three feet of the corner.

For the dog that does not search with purpose, use food on the track at 30, 35, 40, 45, and 50 yards beyond every corner. Keep this up until the dog shows that he clearly anticipates the food sequence and works the corner with a clear purpose. Then start to spread the food out. Finally, slowly and randomly reduce the food so there is typically only one piece about 30 to 45 yards past a corner.

For a dog that does not commit to a new leg as soon as he finds it, or that is tentative in his commitment to a new leg, use the same food sequence as above. It is very important to improve your own clarity of communication and quickness of commitment with these dogs. When the dog begins to anticipate the food sequence ahead, adopt a clear communication sequence between you and dog as he commits to a new leg. When he has moved along the new leg four to ten feet, increase the tension above normal (pull back every so slightly) and verbally ask your dog if this is the good track. The dog should lean into the harness and pull you along the track. The very instant he starts to lean into the harness, you must reduce the tension to normal, step off after your dog, and quietly praise him for being so clever.

Therefore, you have now evaluated your dog in four aspects of being easy or hard to read:

Easy to read. Quick, clear commitment.

Not close to straight legs. Tracks away from the straight legs or weaves widely.

No loss of track at corners. Does not clearly indicate loss of track at a corner.

Weak searching at corners. Does not search with a purpose.

Weakly commits to new leg. Does not commit to new leg quickly and irresistibly.

Here a dog may be classified with multiple symptoms. Choose the highest one in the list.

4.   This question pertains to the handler's ability to read the dog. It requires a great deal of experience to read a dog in any tracking situation. Don't expect to be perfect right away or even with your first dog. Nevertheless, you can become very good if you try. Reread the discussion in Chapter 5 on reading your dog.

If your dog is handling corners well, make the corners blind (no flag, no haystack), but put a flag fifty yards down each leg. Don't look for the flag until you have committed to following the dog. For example, use a wide brimmed hat down over your eyes so you can see no farther in front of you than the dog. Once the dog commits to a new leg, you increase the tension, he pulls into the harness, you reduce the tension and step out, and then you raise your head and verify that the flag is right ahead of you. (If so, pop a small piece of candy in your mouth! If not, back up to the corner and smile.). Keep this up for many sessions until your confidence in your dog increases so that you remain confident when you remove the flags.

If your dog is not handling corners well, he may be being messed up by your lack of confidence. Help the dog become easy to read, then shift into the sequence described above to improve your own confidence.

Therefore, you have now evaluated your own ability to read your dog:

Yes. Read my dog 80% to 100% of the time and believe him quickly and confidently.

No. Read my dog confidently less than 80% of the time on blind corners.

Match your set of answers to one of the rows in the table below:

1 Excitement Level	2 Helped	3 Quick Clear Commit	4 Handler believes Dog	Summary of Plan	Plan / Page
Anticipates or on-track	0 - 1	Easy to read.	Yes	4 TD-like tracks in different locations.	A Page 115
Anticipates or on-track	0 - 1	Easy to read.	No	6-10 TD-like "blind" tracks in different locations with flags 30 yards past corner.	B Page 116
Little excitement	0 - 1	Easy to read.	Yes/No	6-10 TD-like "blind" tracks in different locations with flags 30 yards past corner. Increase motivation.	B Page 116
Anticipates or on-track	2 – 4	Easy to read.	Yes	6-10 TD-like tracks in different locations. Small flag or marker mid-leg. Increase motivation.	A Page 115
Anticipates or on-track	2 - 4	Easy to read.	No	6-10 TD-like "blind" tracks in different locations with flags 30 yards past corner. Increase motivation.	B Page 116
Any	5 or more	Easy to read.	Yes/No	6-10 sessions, 2 tracks/session, 2-corner zigzag tracks with a flag 30 yards past each corner. Increase motivation.	C Page 118
Any	Any	Not close to straight legs.	Yes/No	4-6 sessions, 2 tracks/session, 2-corner zigzag tracks with a flag every 50 yards. Increase motivation, narrow permissible tracking width.	D Page 120
Any	Any	No loss of track at corners	Yes/No	4-6 sessions, 2 tracks/session, 2-corner zigzag tracks with a flag 10 feet before corner. Increase motivation, stay 10 feet behind dog.	E Page 123
Any	Any	Weak searching at corners	Yes/No	6-10 sessions, 2 tracks/session, 2-corner zigzag tracks with drops 30, 35, 40, 45, 50 yards past corners. Increase motivation. Improve communication.	F Page 126
Any	Any	Weakly commits to new leg	Yes/No	6-10 sessions, 2 tracks/session, 2-corner zigzag tracks with drops 30, 35, 40, 45, 50 yards past corners. Increase motivation. Improve communication.	F Page 126

Problem Solving Philosophy

This is a useful place to point out a bit of valuable training philosophy according to Glen Johnson (1977):

> If a dog is not performing in the manner I expect him to perform then I am doing something that has to be wrong. In scent work the dog is the one that knows what he is doing and is always right while the handler, unable to determine just what or how he is doing it, can only set up the situation and hope that it will be conducive to the dogs learning if designed and implemented correctly.

This is a very useful bit of training advice, because it reminds us of who is responsible for what and it also points out the importance of structuring the situation to facilitate learning. This training philosophy should serve as the basis for all problem-solving strategies. The strategy should be designed to allow (and facilitate) the dog to learn the desired behavior. If the dog fails to perform as desired, the problem-solving strategy or our implementation of it is at fault, not the dog.

This training philosophy is very powerful. It is my observation that when a dog is not performing as expected, and I am clever enough to remember the philosophy, then I tend to select or invent other strategies that do teach the desired behavior. However, if I am not clever enough to remember the philosophy and I try to select a strategy based on my own extensive theories of scent, then I get frustrated with the dog's inability to learn what I want. So if you find yourself getting frustrated with your dog, recall this bit of philosophy and see if you cannot find a better way to teach the desired behavior.

Specific Problem Solving Techniques

Do these techniques with Plans C, D, E or F described below or use them with other simple track designs.

- **Poor starts (but the rest of the track is good):** Lay a 50-75 yard straight starter track after laying every track, but run starter before main track. Put a food drop 15 to 45 yards after each start.
- **Weak or no article indication:** Place a marker 20 feet before the article, don't let the dog pass the article, lots of praise and reward for stopping or being stopped. Play the glove game after every track and play it on non-tracking days.
- **Takes animal tracks:** Identify the dog's most favorite reward and restrict access to it except at the end of the track. Lay marked tracks in areas where you think animals may cross your track. Mark the track with a couple of flags on each leg, not necessarily at the corners. If you can predict where animals cross your track, put a food drop 15-30 yards past the area. Put two food drops on every other leg. When the dog tries to take an animal track, let him investigate it 10-40 feet, then move forward down the good track happily calling to your dog something like "Look over here. Is this the good track? Let's find the good track!", and help him down the track a few yards. Be happy and excited and he should start forward along the good track. Help him the rest of the track if need be. Hopefully he will soon come to a delicious food drop and access to his most favorite reward.
- **Distracted by ground animals or birds:** Identify the dog's most favorite reward and restrict access to it except at the end of the track. Lay tracks that cross areas with ground animals or birds. Lead up to this area with easy tracking and exit the area with easy tracking. Use food drops 20, 25, 30, 35, and 40 yards past the area and end track after another 30-50 yards. Let the dog investigate the area briefly, then ask him to return to the main track. Help him happily, if you need to help. Use the most favorite reward at the track end. Repeat for many sessions, but limit distraction area to once per track. If dog refuses to leave distraction, tell him "NO!", then happily help him down the track the rest of the way if you need to.

Plan A Schedule – Polishing Skills in New Fields:

This plan calls for different locations each session. Try several new locations or locations you have not used in a long time. Find sites that are similar to those used to hold tests. You may not be able to find brand new tracking sites, but you should be able to find a few, and different ways to use them, so the dog becomes accustomed to variety.

Session	Location	Turns	Length	Markers	Design	Age
7A.1	New field	3-5	400-500	haystacks	Be creative or choose 5.1, 5.3, 5.5	30
7A.2	New field	3-5	400-500	haystacks	Be creative or choose 6.2, 6.4, 6.6	45
7A.3	New field	3-5	400-500	haystacks	Be creative or choose 6.6, 6.8, 6.10	30
7A.4	New field	3-5	400-500	haystacks	Be creative.	55
7A.5					Evaluate as in 6.11	

Design TD-like tracks that have three-to-five turns and that are 400 to 500 yards long. Be creative in your design but avoid anything very complex. If you want a pre-designed plan, choose one of the sample tracks from the sessions listed. These sessions show two tracks, so do the one that you did not do the first time. Feel free to change the lengths or add an extra leg.

Use subtle markers on corners such as haystacks, ground markers, or nothing at all. Make good maps. Be able to find the track and help the dog if he needs help. If you had to help your dog more than once in the past five TD-like tracks, add a small flag or marker mid-leg to give you confidence that you know where the track is exactly located.

If you have laid all your dog's tracks, find someone else to lay a couple of tracks in this phase. Have them follow 30 yards behind you talking quietly like they were judges following you on a track.

Work on your corner communication. Use extra treats 30 yards after corners if his commitment begins to falter.

Watch your dog's motivation level. If it drops two sessions in a row, back off track difficulty. Reduce difficulty by reducing age, length, number of corners, hilliness of terrain, or increase the familiarity of the fields. If you have even one particularly bad day, add a fun session with a simple marked track on a familiar field.

For the last session, evaluate your dog as you did in session 6.11. If you continue to have a top evaluation, or even if it has dropped a little bit, move right on to Phase 8. Only stop to do some remedial work if the dog has become difficult to read. Otherwise, press right on to the next phase while taking note of what continues to need work.

If the dog develops corner problems and is no longer easy to read, consider remediating with plans C, D, E or F. If the problem is minor, a few sessions may clean it up. Finish off with two or more sessions like those described above and move on to the next phase.

Plan B Schedule – Building Confidence:

This plan calls for different locations each session. Try several new locations or locations you have not used in a long time. Find sites that are similar to those used to hold tests. You may not be able to find brand new tracking sites, but you should be able to find a few, and different ways to use them, so the dog becomes accustomed to variety.

Session	Location	Turns	Length	Markers	Design	Age
7B.1	New field	3-5	400-500	Flag 30 past corner	Be creative or choose 5.1, 5.3	30
7B.2	New field	3-5	400-500	Flag 30 past corner	Be creative or choose 5.2, 5.4	45
7B.3	New field	3-5	400-500	Flag 30 past corner	Be creative or choose 5.5, 5.6	30
7B.4	New field	3-5	400-500	Flag 30 past corner	Be creative or choose 6.2, 6.4	50
7B.5	New field	3-5	400-500	Flag 30 past corner	Be creative or choose 6.6, 6.8	35
7B.6	New field	3-5	400-500	Flag 30 past corner	Be creative or choose 5.2, 6.10	40
7B.7*	New field	3-5	400-500	Flag 30 past corner	Be creative or choose 5.4, 6.8	30
7B.8*	New field	3-5	400-500	Flag 30 past corner	Be creative or choose 5.6, 6.6	50
7B.9*	New field	3-5	400-500	Flag 30 past corner	Be creative or choose 5.5, 6.4	35
7B.10*	New field	3-5	400-500	Flag 30 past corner	Be creative.	30
7B.11					Evaluate as in 6.11	

Design TD-like tracks that have three-to-five turns and that are 400 to 500 yards long. Be creative in your design but avoid anything very complex. If you want a pre-designed plan, choose one of the sample tracks from the sessions listed. These sessions show two tracks, so do the one that you did not do the first time. Feel free to change the lengths or add an extra leg.

Use a flag 30 yards past every corner. Use subtle markers on corners such as haystacks, ground markers, or nothing at all. Make good maps. Be able to find the track and help the dog if he needs help.

If you have laid all your dog's tracks, find someone else to lay a couple of tracks in this phase. Have them follow 30 yards behind you talking quietly like they were judges following you on a track.

Work on your corner communication. Use extra treats 30 yards after corners if his commitment begins to falter.

Watch your dog's motivation level. If it is not as high as you want it to be, upgrade your motivational techniques. If the dog's motivation drops two sessions in a row, back off track difficulty. Reduce difficulty by reducing age, length, number of corners, hilliness of terrain, or increase the familiarity of the fields. If you have one particularly bad day, add a fun session with a simple marked track on a familiar field.

If after session 7B.6 your dog is doing very well, evaluate your dog as in session 6.11. If the evaluation is excellent, move on to phase 8 without finishing this phase. If it is not much better than the previous evaluation, continue with this phase.

For the last session, evaluate your dog as you did in session 6.11. If you continue to have a top evaluation, or even if it has dropped a little bit, move right on to Phase 8. Only stop to do some remedial work if the dog has become difficult to read. Otherwise, press right on to the next phase while keeping track of what continues to need work.

If the dog develops corner problems and is no longer easy to read, consider remediating with plans C, D, E or F. If the problem is minor, a few sessions may clean it up. Finish off with two or more sessions like those described above and move on to the next phase.

Plan C Schedule – Skill Development:

Session	Tracks	Turns	Length	Markers	Design	Age
7C.1	2 zigzags	2x2	400-500	Flag 30 past corner	2 simple zigzag tracks	30
7C.2	2 zigzags	2x2	400-500	Flag 30 past corner	2 simple zigzag tracks	45
7C.3	2 zigzags	2x2	400-500	Flag 30 past corner	2 simple zigzag tracks	30
7C.4	2 zigzags	2x2	400-500	Flag 30 past corner	2 simple zigzag tracks	50
7C.5	2 zigzags	2x2	400-500	Flag 30 past corner	2 simple zigzag tracks	35
7C.6	2 zigzags	2x2	400-500	Flag 30 past corner	2 simple zigzag tracks	40
7C.7	TD-like	3-5	400-500	Flag 30 past corner	Be creative or choose 5.3, 6.4	30
7C.8	TD-like	3-5	400-500	Flag 30 past corner	Be creative or choose 5.4, 6.6	50
7C.9	TD-like	3-5	400-500	Flag 30 past corner	Be creative or choose 5.5, 6.8	35
7C.10	TD-like	3-5	400-500	Flag 30 past corner	Be creative or choose 5.6, 6.10	30
7C.11					Evaluate as in 6.11	

Unlike plans A and B, this plan does not expect you to find new tracking fields each day. If things are going well, make a couple of these sessions on new tracking fields. Find sites that are similar to those used to hold tests. You may not be able to find brand new tracking sites, but you should be able to find different ways to use them, so the dog becomes accustomed to variety.

A zigzag track is a two-corner track like those seen in phase 4. A sample is shown below which can be used for the first six sessions by adjusting the lengths of the leg. If your tracking field has trouble accommodating two zigzags, make one of them a U shaped track (both corners or in the same direction like the tracks in 6.1, 6.3, ...).

For the last four sessions, design TD-like tracks that have three-to-five turns and that are 400 to 500 yards long. Be creative in your design but avoid anything very complex. If you want a pre-designed plan, choose one of the sample tracks from the sessions listed. These sessions show two tracks, so do the one that you did not do the first time. Feel free to change the lengths or add an extra leg.

Use a flag 30 yards past every corner. Use subtle markers on corners such as haystacks, ground markers, or nothing at all. Make good maps. Be able to find the track and help the dog if he needs help. If dog starts to key into flags when finding the next leg, put a flag 20 yards before the corner and another flag mid-leg. To minimize confusion while running the track, use different types of flags before the corner and mid-leg.

If you have laid all your dog's tracks, find someone else to lay a couple of tracks in this phase. Have them follow 30 yards behind you talking quietly like they were judges following you on a track.

Work on your corner communication. Use extra treats 30-50 yards after corners if his commitment begins to falter.

Watch your dog's motivation level. If it is not as high as you want it to be, upgrade your motivational techniques. If it drops two sessions in a row, back off track difficulty. Reduce difficulty by reducing age, length, number of corners, hilliness of terrain, or increase the familiarity of the fields. If you have even one particularly bad day, add a fun session with a simple marked track on a familiar field.

For the last session, evaluate your dog as you did in session 6.11. If you continue to have a top-notch evaluation or if it has just dropped a little bit, move right on to Phase 8. Only stop to do some remedial work if the dog has become difficult to read. Otherwise, press right on to the next phase while keeping track of what continues to need work.

If the dog develops corner problems and is no longer easy to read, consider remediating with plans D, E or F. If the problem is minor, a few sessions may clean it up. Finish off with two or more sessions like those described above and move on to the next phase.

Session 7C.(1-6)

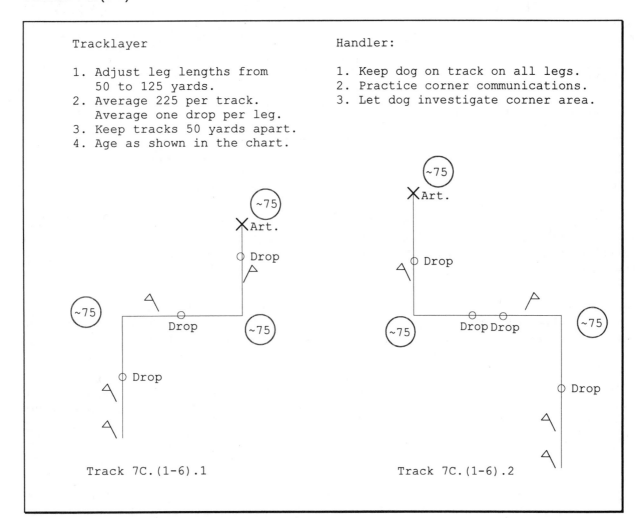

```
      Tracklayer                        Handler:

      1. Adjust leg lengths from        1. Keep dog on track on all legs.
         50 to 125 yards.               2. Practice corner communications.
      2. Average 225 per track.         3. Let dog investigate corner area.
         Average one drop per leg.
      3. Keep tracks 50 yards apart.
      4. Age as shown in the chart.
```

Track 7C.(1-6).1   Track 7C.(1-6).2

Plan D Schedule – Improving Line Tracking Skills:

This plan is for dogs that do not track straight down the line of footsteps.

Session	Tracks	Turns	Length	Markers	Design	Age
7D.1	2 zigzags	2x2	400-500	Flag 30 past corner	2 simple zigzag tracks	30
7D.2	2 zigzags	2x2	400-500	Flag 30 past corner	2 simple zigzag tracks	45
7D.3	2 zigzags	2x2	400-500	Flag 30 past corner	2 simple zigzag tracks	30
7D.4	2 zigzags	2x2	400-500	Flag 30 past corner	2 simple zigzag tracks	50
7D.4a					Evaluate "close to track?"	
7D.5*	2 zigzags	2x2	400-500	Flag 30 past corner	2 simple zigzag tracks	35
7D.6*	2 zigzags	2x2	400-500	Flag 30 past corner	2 simple zigzag tracks	40
7D.6a					Evaluate "close to track?"	
7D.7*	TD-like	3-5	400-500	Flag 30 past corner	Be creative or choose 5.3, 6.4	30
7D.8*	TD-like	3-5	400-500	Flag 30 past corner	Be creative or choose 5.4, 6.6	50
7D.9*	TD-like	3-5	400-500	Flag 30 past corner	Be creative or choose 5.5, 6.8	35
7D.10*	TD-like	3-5	400-500	Flag 30 past corner	Be creative or choose 5.6, 6.10	30
7D.11					Evaluate as in 6.11	

* Use starred sessions only if recommended by evaluation. See the text below.

Unlike plans A and B, this plan does not expect you to find new tracking fields each day. If things are going well, make a couple of these sessions on new tracking fields. Find sites that are similar to those used to hold tests. You may not be able to find brand new tracking sites, but you should be able to find different ways to use them, so the dog becomes accustomed to variety.

A zigzag track is a two-corner track like those worked in phase 4. A sample is shown below which can be used for the first six sessions by adjusting the lengths of the legs. If your tracking field has trouble accommodating two zigzags, make one of them a U shaped track (both corners or in the same direction like the tracks in 6.1, 6.3, …).

After session 4 and 6, evaluate the progress your dog has made in staying close to the track. If you have seen improvement and there are other hard-to-read issues such as lack of purpose when searching, now is the time to switch to Plan E or F as appropriate. Remember to keep him close to the straight legs in all future tracks as four to six sessions is not enough to completely cure the problem. Nevertheless, you should be able to combine your straight-leg work with your corner remediation.

If you have not seen much improvement, you need to get creative. Did you really do a good job in Phase 1 and 2? Are you keeping a nice comfortable tension the whole time? What do you think causes this particular dog to stray so far from the track? A dog that anticipates a cool reward coming up along this smelly line of footprints should be quite efficient getting to it. Consider motivational issues. Reflect critically on these issues and design a plan that addresses them. There is probably little point in continuing with sessions 7 through 10. You will probably benefit more from simpler marked tracks with a significant focus on lead handling and an improved system of motivational rewards.

If you have seen improvement in sessions one through six and there are no other hard-to-read issues, continue with sessions 7 through 10 and then repeat your evaluation of session 6.11 based on these more recent tracks. Proceed based on this new evaluation.

For the last four sessions, design TD-like tracks that have three-to-five turns and that are 400 to 500 yards long. Be creative in your design but avoid anything very complex. If you want a pre-designed plan, choose one of the sample tracks from the sessions listed. These sessions show two tracks, so do the one that you did not do the first time. Feel free to change the lengths or add an extra leg.

Use a flag 30 yards past every corner on these TD-like tracks. Use subtle markers on corners such as haystacks, ground markers, or nothing at all. Make good maps. Be able to find the track and help the dog if he needs help. If dog starts to key into flags when finding the next leg, put a flag 20 yards before the corner and another flag mid-leg. To minimize confusion when running the track, use different types of flags before the corner and mid-leg.

If you have laid all your dog's tracks, find someone else to lay a couple of tracks in this phase. Have them follow 30 yards behind you talking quietly like they were judges following you on a track.

Work on your corner communication. Use extra treats 30-50 yards after corners if his commitment begins to falter.

Watch your dog's motivation level. If it is not as high as you want it to be, upgrade your motivational techniques. If it drops two sessions in a row, back off track difficulty. Reduce difficulty by reducing age, length, number of corners, hilliness of terrain, or increase the familiarity of the fields. If you have even one particularly bad day, add a fun session with a simple marked track on a familiar field.

For the last session, evaluate your dog as you did in session 6.11. If you continue to have a top-notch evaluation or if it has just dropped a little bit, move right on to Phase 8. Only stop to do some remedial work if the dog has become difficult to read. Otherwise, press right on to the next phase while keeping track of what continues to need work.

If the dog develops corner problems and is no longer easy to read, consider remediating with plans D, E or F. If the problem is minor, a few sessions may clean it up. Finish off with two or more sessions like those described above and move on to the next phase.

Tracklayer

1. Adjust leg lengths from
   50 to 125 yards.
2. Average 225 per track.
   Average one drop per leg.
3. Flags every 50 yards, but
   not right on the corners.
4. Keep tracks 50 yards apart.
5. Age as shown in the chart.

Handler:

1. Keep dog on track on all legs.
2. Practice corner communications.
3. Let dog investigate corner area.

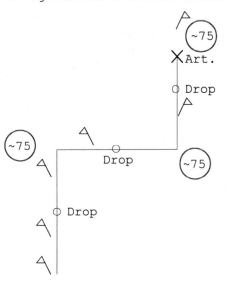

Track 7D.(1-6).1

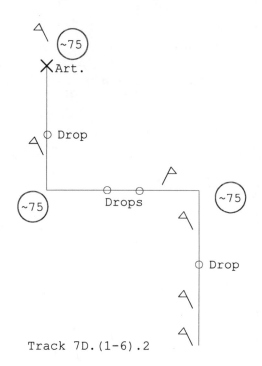

Track 7D.(1-6).2

Plan E Schedule – Increasing the Dog's Corner Indication:

This plan is for dogs that overshoot the corner substantially; that is, for the dog that does not indicate loss of scent shortly after passing the corner.

Session	Tracks	Turns	Length	Markers	Design	Age
7E.1	2 zigzags	2x2	400-500	Flag 10' before corner	2 simple zigzag tracks	30
7E.2	2 zigzags	2x2	400-500	Flag 10' before corner	2 simple zigzag tracks	45
7E.3	2 zigzags	2x2	400-500	Flag 10' before corner	2 simple zigzag tracks	30
7E.4	2 zigzags	2x2	400-500	Flag 10' before corner	2 simple zigzag tracks	50
7E.4a					Evaluate "close to track?"	
7E.5*	2 zigzags	2x2	400-500	Flag 10' before corner	2 simple zigzag tracks	35
7E.6*	2 zigzags	2x2	400-500	Flag 10' before corner	2 simple zigzag tracks	40
7E.6a					Evaluate "close to track?"	
7E.7*	TD-like	3-5	400-500	Flag 10' before corner	Be creative or choose 5.3, 6.4	30
7E.8*	TD-like	3-5	400-500	Flag 10' before corner	Be creative or choose 5.4, 6.6	50
7E.9*	TD-like	3-5	400-500	Flag 10' before corner	Be creative or choose 5.5, 6.8	35
7E.10*	TD-like	3-5	400-500	Flag 10' before corner	Be creative or choose 5.6, 6.10	30
7E.11					Evaluate as in 6.11	

* Use starred sessions only if recommended by evaluation. See the text below.

Unlike plans A and B, this plan does not expect you to find new tracking fields each day. If things are going well, make a couple of these sessions on new tracking fields. Find sites that are similar to those used to hold tests. You may not be able to find brand new tracking sites, but you should be able to find different ways to use them, so the dog becomes accustomed to variety.

A zigzag track is a two-corner track similar to those worked in phase 4. A sample is shown below which can be used for the first six sessions by adjusting the lengths of the legs. If your tracking field has trouble accommodating two zigzags, make one of them a U shaped track (both corners or in the same direction like the tracks in 6.1, 6.3, …).

After session 4 and 6, evaluate the progress your dog has made in staying close to the track. If you have seen improvement and there are other hard-to-read issues such as lack of purpose when searching, now is the time to switch to Plan F. Remember to keep him close to the corner in all future tracks as four to six sessions is not enough to completely cure the problem. Nevertheless, you should be able to combine your loss of scent recognition work with your corner remediation.

If you have not seen much improvement, you need to get creative. Did you really do a good job in Phase 1 and 2? Are you keeping a nice comfortable tension the whole time? What do you think causes this particular dog to overrun the corners so far? A dog that anticipates a cool reward coming up along these smelly lines of footprints should be quite efficient recognizing when one line of footprints stops and another starts in a new direction. Consider motivational issues. Reflect critically on these issues and design a plan that addresses them. There is probably little point in continuing with sessions 7 through 10. You will probably benefit more from simpler marked tracks with a significant focus on lead handling and an improved system of motivational rewards.

If you have seen improvement in sessions one through six and there are no other hard-to-read issues, continue with sessions 7 through 10 and then repeat your evaluation of session 6.11 based on these more recent tracks. Proceed based on this new evaluation.

For the last four sessions, design TD-like tracks that have three-to-five turns and that are 400 to 500 yards long. Be creative in your design but avoid anything very complex. If you want a pre-designed plan, choose one of the sample tracks from the sessions listed. These sessions show two tracks, so do the one that you did not do the first time. Feel free to change the lengths or add an extra leg.

Use a flag 10 feet before every corner on these TD-like tracks. Make good maps. Be able to find the track and help the dog if he needs help.

Work on your corner communication. Use extra treats 30-50 yards after corners if his commitment begins to falter.

Watch your dog's motivation level. If it is not as high as you want it to be, upgrade your motivational techniques. If it drops two sessions in a row, back off track difficulty. Reduce difficulty by reducing age, length, number of corners, hilliness of terrain, or increase the familiarity of the fields. If you have even one particularly bad day, add a fun session with a simple marked track on a familiar field.

For the last session, evaluate your dog as you did in session 6.11. If you have an excellent evaluation, move right on to Phase 8. Only stop to do more remedial work if the dog is still difficult to read. Otherwise, press right on to the next phase while keeping track of what continues to need work.

If the dog continues to exhibit corner problems or develops new corner problems and is not easy to read, consider remediating with plans C, D, or F. If the problem is minor, a few sessions may clean it up. Finish off with two or more sessions like those described above and move on to the next phase.

Tracklayer

1. Adjust leg lengths from
   50 to 125 yards.
2. Average 225 per track.
   Average one drop per leg.
3. A flag 10 feet before each
   corner.
4. Keep tracks 50 yards apart.
5. Age as shown in the chart.

Handler:

1. Keep dog on track on all legs.
2. Practice corner communications.
3. Let dog investigate corner area.

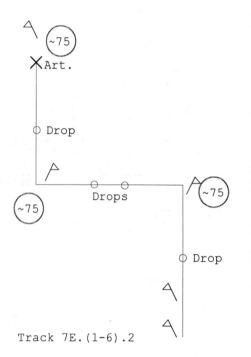

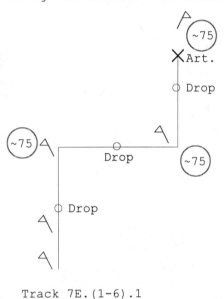

Track 7E.(1-6).1

Track 7E.(1-6).2

Plan F Schedule – Improving the Dog's Corner Motivation:

This plan is for dogs that do not search for new legs purposefully and efficiently, or for dogs who fail to quickly commit to a new leg or who commit only weakly.

Session	Tracks	Turns	Length	Markers	Design	Age
7F.1	2 zigzags	2x2	400-500	Flag 30 past corner	2 simple zigzag tracks	30
7F.2	2 zigzags	2x2	400-500	Flag 30 past corner	2 simple zigzag tracks	45
7F.3	2 zigzags	2x2	400-500	Flag 30 past corner	2 simple zigzag tracks	30
7F.4	2 zigzags	2x2	400-500	Flag 30 past corner	2 simple zigzag tracks	50
7F.5	2 zigzags	2x2	400-500	Flag 30 past corner	2 simple zigzag tracks	35
7F.6	2 zigzags	2x2	400-500	Flag 30 past corner	2 simple zigzag tracks	40
7F.7	TD-like	3-5	400-500	Flag 30 past corner	Be creative or choose 5.3, 6.4	30
7F.8	TD-like	3-5	400-500	Flag 30 past corner	Be creative or choose 5.4, 6.6	50
7F.9	TD-like	3-5	400-500	Flag 30 past corner	Be creative or choose 5.5, 6.8	35
7F.10	TD-like	3-5	400-500	Flag 30 past corner	Be creative or choose 5.6, 6.10	30
7F.11					Evaluate as in 6.11	

Unlike plans A and B, this plan does not expect you to find new tracking fields each day. If things are going well, make a couple of these sessions on new tracking fields. Find sites that are similar to those used to hold tests. You may not be able to find brand new tracking sites, but you should be able to find different ways to use them, so the dog becomes accustomed to variety.

A zigzag track is a two-corner track similar to those seen in phase 4. A sample is shown below which can be used for the first six sessions by adjusting the lengths of the leg. If your tracking field has trouble accommodating two zigzags, make one of them a U shaped track (both corners or in the same direction like the tracks in 6.1, 6.3, …).

For the last four sessions, design TD-like tracks that have three-to-five turns and that are 400 to 500 yards long. Be creative in your design but avoid anything very complex. If you want a pre-designed plan, choose one of the sample tracks from the sessions listed. These sessions show two tracks, so do the one that you did not do the first time. Feel free to change the lengths or add an extra leg.

Use a sequence of food drops 30, 35, 40, 45, and 50 yards past every corner. Continue at least 30 yards past the last food drop before making the next corner or ending the track. This means that the legs must be 80 or more yards long except the first one that can be shorter.

This food sequence is very effective for getting the dog to anticipate that something good is coming up after the corner. It may take several sessions for this anticipation to take hold, but it should be very noticeable by the third to sixth session. Once this anticipation become consistent, randomly increase the distance between the 5 drops and reduce the number of drops. Over four to six more sessions, you should be able to reduce the food to one or two pieces per leg. If the dog's anticipation reduces, you have reduced the food drops to quickly. Go back, add all five, and then withdraw them more slowly.

Dogs that are slow to find and commit to a new leg often are slow to start a track. You will notice a food drop at 15 yards on the start to encourage the dog to get started faster. As you notice the dog start each track more quickly, move this food drop farther from the start. If your dog is a very slow starter, but tracks OK once he gets started, put an additional food sequence starting at 35 of the first leg as well as the extra drop at 15 yards.

Use a flag about mid-leg. Use subtle markers on corners such as haystacks, ground markers, or nothing at all. Make good maps. Be able to find the track and help the dog if he needs help.

Work on your corner communication. Once the dog anticipates the sequence of five food drops, he should really pull you off the corner. It is very important to improve your own clarity of communication and quickness of commitment with these dogs. When the dog begins to anticipate the food sequence ahead, adopt a clear communication sequence between you and dog as he commits to a new leg. When he has moved along the new leg four to ten feet, increase the tension above normal (pull back every so slightly) and verbally ask your dog "Is this is the good track?" The dog should lean into the harness and pull you along the track. The very instant he starts to lean into the harness, you must reduce the tension to normal, step off after your dog, and quietly praise him for being so clever.

When increasing the tension as you ask the dog "Is this the good track?" make sure you do not jerk the dog. Smoothly and evenly, increase the tension slightly. If the dog is right on the track, and he anticipates having a good time further down the track, he will lean into the harness. Immediately reduce the tension to normal and step off down the track! On the other hand, if the dog is not right on the track, he will be reminded to look for the good track and will veer off to do so. You will not see the dog lean into the harness so you will not step off the corner.

Watch your dog's motivation level. If it is not as high as you want it to be, upgrade your motivational techniques. If it drops two sessions in a row, back off track difficulty. Reduce difficulty by reducing age, length, number of corners, hilliness of terrain, or increase the familiarity of the fields. If you have even one particularly bad day, add a fun session with a simple marked track on a familiar field.

For the last session, evaluate your dog as you did in session 6.11. If you continue to have a top-notch evaluation or if it has just dropped a little bit, move right on to Phase 8. Only stop to do some remedial work if the dog has become difficult to read. Otherwise, press right on to the next phase while keeping track of what continues to need work.

If the dog develops corner problems and is no longer easy to read, consider remediating with plans D, E or F. If the problem is minor, a few sessions may clean it up. Finish off with two or more sessions like those described above and move on to the next phase.

Tracklayer

1. Adjust leg lengths from
   50 to 125 yards.
2. Average 225 per track.
3. Five drops after corners,
   at 30, 35, 40, 45, and 50.
4. Keep tracks 50 yards apart.
5. Age as shown in the chart.

Handler:

1. Keep dog on track on all legs.
2. Practice corner communications.
3. Let dog investigate corner area.

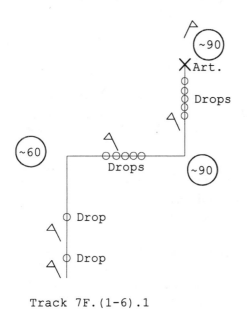

Track 7F.(1-6).1

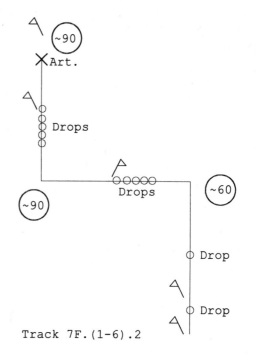

Track 7F.(1-6).2

Phase 8. Preparing for the Test.

Purpose:

- Prepare you and your dog for the Tracking Dog test.

Strategy:

- Familiarize you and your dog with test-like terrain and tracking conditions.
- Teach your dog to ignore some common handler errors.
- Peak your dog's performance for the test.
- (Optional) Teach your dog to track 2-hour-old tracks while ignoring 24-hour-old tracks.

Tracking Tests

Tracking tests are different from most other dog events because of the limited number of dogs who can enter any one event. It typically takes two judges and five to ten helpers two full days to put on a single test for twelve dogs. So tracking tests are organized a little differently from dog shows or obedience trials. In AKC tests, you need a certification that your dog is ready in order to enter a test. Some tests have many more entrants than tracks, so different systems have evolved for determining which entrants get into the test. For an AKC test, all entrants are randomly drawn after the closing date to determine who gets in. In Canada, the first entries to arrive at the secretary's mailbox are the ones who get into the test. The rulebook should help you learn how the entries are taken.

I hope that you get into the test you enter. However, if you become an alternate, attend the test anyway. If one of the regular dogs fails to show up, or gets sick, the alternates are offered the track in the order they were drawn at the closing. Even if you do not get into the test, you will get to see some of the dogs run and become more familiar with the way tests are run. Be sure to verify that the test-like tracks you have been plotting for your dog in training match the complexity of the tracks you see at the test.

In fact, it is a good idea to watch a tracking test before you enter just so you will be familiar with the way thing happen at a test. Feel free to lay tracks for a test before you are ready to enter one. If you have a suitable vehicle, offer to provide transportation for the tracklayers and handlers between the tracking fields.

You will find a description of what to do on the day of your test on page 134 below. In the next section, you will find the training program to follow to be prepared for your test day.

Preparation Processes:

Now that you have a well prepared and skillful tracking dog, and now that you are a well prepared and skillful handler, there are only a few more details to consider as your approach your dog's TD test. We will consider each of the pre-test issues and then you will plan your training accordingly.

Certification was mentioned in Chapters 5, 6 and 7. If you are preparing for an AKC test, you will need to be certified by an AKC judge as ready to enter a test. This is done by having a judge put you through a TD test-like track. So if you are not already certified, go ahead and get it done.

Look ahead at the calendar for the next few tracking tests and decide which you will enter. That decision generates your timeline and allows you to plan the number of training sessions that can be worked between now and the test.

Site Familiarity. It is my experience that dogs and handlers who are familiar with a tracking test site are more likely to pass than those who are unfamiliar with the site. The dirt and vegetation at each site probably smells a little different to the dog. In addition, it is quite common for a site to harbor some unusual flora or fauna that may distract the dog when it tracks at a site for the first time. So, when you enter a TD test, try to find out as much as you can about the test site.

Can you track there before the test? Many tests are held at public parks that allow you to track. However, many tests are held at private or restricted sites that allow tests but do not allow the public access. Avoid using the actual site the week before the test even if it is available for public use. If you cannot use the actual site, find a similar site – one that is likely to have the same sort of micro-ecology as the actual test site.

I personally try to track at a test site (or a similar substitute) two to four times before a test. If my dog and I are comfortable after two sessions, we leave it at that. Nevertheless, it is good to allow time for up to four sessions in case there are problems the first time or two at the site. I once tracked at a test site a few weeks before a test and discovered that my dog was totally distracted by what the geese left behind as they foraged there. This site was several hours from my home, so it took considerable effort to get back there several more times to get him completely comfortable with the site. Since I was willing to drive several hours to the test, I had to be willing to drive several hours to prepare for it. He ended up drawing the hill that the geese favored and passing the test. You will not know what you are unprepared for until you actually track at the site, so go to the extra effort to do so.

Proofing handler errors. Almost all handlers make handling mistakes in tests. The handler gets nervous and does something that they would not ordinarily do. It is so likely to happen in a test that I like to expose my dog to the experience of handler error so that he learns to continue on the track in spite of it. These proofing sessions are set up to allow you to act stupid on a couple of corners and be assured that the dog will be highly rewarded as soon as he overcomes your stupidity.

Peaking performance for the test. You can do a few things in the last couple of weeks before a test to make sure that the dog's skill and enthusiasm for tracking is at its peak. The general idea is to work the dog quite hard two to three weeks before a test, then back off to motivational tracks the first half of the pre-test week, followed by a layoff for 3-4 days before the test.

Aging to two-hour-old tracks (Optional). Up until now, we have avoided teaching the dog to track past about one hour because they tend to become quite interested in 24-hour-old tracks once they learn to track 90-120 minute old tracks. Unfortunately, the way tracks are plotted out the day before a test makes it likely that your dog will have to distinguish his test track from a false track made on plotting day. Once you teach a dog to follow a 2-hour-old track, you also must teach him to correctly distinguish the original track from 24-hour old tracks. This is not hard to do, but it does take a little extra time and effort.

The idea is to increase the age of the tracks in 10-minute increments from 60 minutes to 120 minutes. Use TD-like tracks and intersperse the aged track sessions with an occasional 30-minute-old motivational track. Use enough 30-minute-old fun tracks to keep your dog's enthusiasm up even if he has a little difficulty learning to follow the older tracks.

Once this first step is done and your dog seems comfortable tracking 2-hour-old tracks, you set up pairs of days that you can track in the same place. The first day, you lay a TD track in the field just as usual. You make a very good map and become thoroughly familiar with the landmarks in the field. You may even leave a few pieces of surveyor's tape in strategic locations along the track overnight. The next day, you lay a different TD-like track that crisscrosses the first track in known places. Be sure to leave a couple of nice food drops 5 to 20 yards past the places the tracks cross. If your dog notices yesterday's track, allow him to investigate it. If the dog tries to commit to the wrong track for more than 10-15 feet, move up the correct track past where they cross and happily call your dog to find the good track. Point at the good track, be very happy, be very excited about this good track, and your dog will quickly get the idea and get the food drops you left.

You may need to repeat this double day process three to six times to allow your dog to understand the concept and learn to stay with the original track.

Track Age Schedule (optional):

This plan is for dog-handler teams with enough time before their test to complete the whole track age schedule as well as the test preparation schedule. If you do not have time to do both, skip this track age schedule and go on to the test preparation schedule. This twenty-one session schedule takes two to three months to complete assuming you track two to three times a week.

Session	Location	Turns	Length	Markers	Design	Age
8A.1	Anyplace	3-5	400-500	Haystacks	TD-like	1:00
8A.2	Anyplace	3-5	400-500	Haystacks	TD-like	1:10
8A.3	Anyplace	3-5	400-500	Haystacks	TD-like	1:20
8A.4	Anyplace	3-5	400-500	Haystacks	TD-like	30
8A.5	Anyplace	3-5	400-500	Haystacks	TD-like	1:30
8A.6	Anyplace	3-5	400-500	Haystacks	TD-like	1:40
8A.7	Anyplace	3-5	400-500	Haystacks	TD-like	1:50
8A.8	Anyplace	3-5	400-500	Haystacks	TD-like	45
8A.9	Anyplace	3-5	400-500	Haystacks	TD-like	2:00
8A.10	Site A	3-5	400-500	Haystacks +	Fun TD-like	1:30
8A.11	Site A – Next Day	3-5	400-500	Haystacks	TD-like / Crisscross	1:00
8A.12	Fun familiar site	3-5	400-500	Haystacks	TD-like	30
8A.13	Site B	3-5	400-500	Haystacks +	TD-like	1:45
8A.14	Site B – Next Day	3-5	400-500	Haystacks	TD-like / Crisscross	1:15
8A.15	Fun familiar site	3-5	400-500	Haystacks	Fun TD-like	45
8A.16	Site C	3-5	400-500	Haystacks +	TD-like	2:00
8A.17	Site C – Next Day	3-5	400-500	Haystacks	TD-like / Crisscross	1:30
8A.18	Fun familiar site	3-5	400-500	Haystacks	Fun TD-like	30
8A.19	Site D	3-5	400-500	Haystacks +	TD-like	2:15
8A.20	Site D – Next Day	3-5	400-500	Haystacks	TD-like / Crisscross	1:45
8A.21	Fun familiar site	3-5	400-500	Haystacks	Fun TD-like	45

Design TD-like tracks that have three-to-five turns and that are 400 to 500 yards long. Be creative in your design but avoid anything very complex.

Use subtle markers on corners such as haystacks, ground markers, or nothing at all. Make good maps. Be able to find the track and help the dog if he needs help. If you had to help your dog more than once in the past five TD-like tracks, add a small flag or marker mid-leg to give you confidence that you know where the track is exactly located. For the first day of the two-day session pairs (8A.10, 8A.13, 8A.16, 8A.19), leave some surveyors tape on the track to help you be sure of the landmarks and where tomorrow's track can cross today's.

Continue to work on your corner communication and keeping the dog close to the straight legs. Use extra treats 30 yards after corners if his commitment begins to falter.

Watch your dog's motivation level. If it drops two sessions in a row, back off track difficulty. Reduce difficulty by reducing length, number of corners, hilliness of terrain, or increase the familiarity of the fields. If you have even one particularly bad day, add a fun session with a simple marked track on a familiar field.

For the second day of the two-day paired sessions (8A.11, 8A.14, 8A.17 or 8A.20), if your dog notices yesterday's track, allow him to investigate it. If the dog tries to commit to the wrong track for more than 10-15 feet, move up the correct track past where they cross and happily call your dog to find the good track. Point at the good track, be very happy, be very excited about this good track, and your dog will quickly get the idea and get the food drops you left.

If your dog is still committing to yesterday's tracks by the end of this schedule, add a few more sessions in the three-session pattern of 8A.10 through 8A.21. However, I expect your dog is beginning to get the idea about staying on the track that we started on.

Test Preparation Schedule:

This plan is for dog-handler teams who are preparing for a test. Feel free to adjust this to fit you and your dog's particular needs. As the test approaches, do the last three sessions on the days indicated and avoid tracking or other strenuous activity for your dog on the four days before the test.

Session	Location	Turns	Length	Markers	Design	Age
8P.1	Fun familiar site	5-6	400-500	Flags mid-leg	Proof Handler Errors	30
8P.2	Test-like site	3-5	400-500	Flags mid-leg	TD-like	20
8P.3	Fun familiar site	5-6	400-500	Flags mid-leg	Proof Handler Errors	45
8P.4	Test-like site	3-5	400-500	Haystacks	TD-like	30
8P.5	Fun familiar site	5-6	400-500	Flags mid-leg	Proof Handler Errors	60
8P.6	Test-like site	3-5	400-500	Haystacks	TD-like	45
8P.7	Anyplace 8 days before test	4-6	500-600	Haystacks	TD-like Long but fun	50
8P.8	Anyplace 7 days before test	4-6	500-600	Haystacks	TD-like Long but fun	45
8P.9	Fun familiar site 5 days before test	3-5	250	Haystacks	Short Easy Fun	30

For sessions one through six, design TD-like tracks that have three-to-six turns and that are 400 to 500 yards long. Be creative in your design but avoid anything very complex. Use subtle markers on corners such as haystacks, ground markers, or nothing at all. Make good maps. Be able to find the track and help the dog if he needs help.

If you are traveling a long distance out of your area to a test, you may be unable to arrive at the test area until just a few days before the test. The earlier you can arrive, the better; but few of us can arrive at a national specialty tracking test two weeks before the event in order to follow the 8P schedule above. Talk to the test secretary or someone local to the test site who is familiar with the site and get a good description of the site. Find someplace near your home that approximates the site and track there. When you get to the test area, walk your dog around in another area similar to the test site, and then give your dog the following sequence of tracks: A 50 yard straight track 15-minutes-old, an 70x50 yard single corner "L" track 25-minutes-old, and a 75x75x50 zigzag track 35-minutes-old. If you think your dog might take more than 10 minutes to run a track, lay them one at a time. Don't use the test site for these last minute tracks unless you are there more than 5 days before the test.

Proofing Handler Errors Sessions

For the sessions where you will proof handler errors, look at the track and select two or three easy corners to do your proofing. Make sure there are two food drops 30 and 35 yards past these corners. Common handler errors are:

 Unusually high tension when dog commits to the new leg.
 Line goes slack while dog is searching.
 Follow dog in an uncertain/disbelieving manner with a slack line or a very tight line.
 Inadvertently stand on the line as dog commits to new leg.
 Stand your ground and refuse to follow the dog on the new leg the first time he tries to commit.

Each session, select one or more of these common handler errors and act it out on those corners. Be as much of a ham as you need to be to put the dog off a little bit. Once the dog reacts to your acting, stop acting and return to your normal handling.

If the dog quits searching, help him with the correct track. Be very happy and upbeat about showing him the track and encouraging him to find it. If the dog continues to search but fails to take the new leg the next time he crosses it, help him as described above. If the dog continues to search but avoids returning to the area of the new leg in a few minutes, help him as described above.

As the dog tracks the next leg, watch his attitude. Wait to proof another handler error until his enthusiastic attitude returns to normal. It may take another corner or two for him to regain confidence in his teammate who seems to be having a very off day.

Watch your dog's motivation level. If it drops two sessions in a row, back off track difficulty. Reduce difficulty by reducing age, length, number of corners, hilliness of terrain, or increase the familiarity of the fields. If you have even one particularly bad day, add a fun session with a simple marked track on a familiar field.

The Day of the Test

On the day of the test, arrive early for the draw where the dogs' running order is determined. The time and location of the draw is indicated on the premium list and judging schedule for the test.

If I am unfamiliar with the test site, I may drive by the site the night before the test to make sure I can find it. I typically arrive about a half-hour before the draw, so I have plenty of time to get lost, put on my boots, and exercise my dog before the draw. Typically, the dog that runs first will be at his start about fifteen to twenty minutes after the draw, so you should be prepared. On the other hand, the dog who runs twelfth in a twelve dog test may have to wait three to four hours after the draw before getting to start his track.

When it is your turn, you may be able to walk to your track, you may be able to drive someplace near it, or you may have to ride in a stranger's truck to get to your track. However you get there, you will meet two judges who, despite their perhaps imposing demeanor, are rooting for you to pass just as much as you are hoping to pass. They will tell you where the track starts and when you can start it.

By the time you get to the test, you and your dog are very well prepared to pass. Unless some very unusual distraction occurs, or unless you completely forget all your handling and communication skills, you and your dog will pass. You probably cannot do anything about very unusual distractions but your training up to now has gotten you ready for all usual distractions and many unusual ones. You can remind yourself that you need only to read your dog, trust him, communicate with him your confidence in his skill and follow him. You know how to do all these things, so you can relax and just do them.

If your dog gets into trouble on the track, organize his search. Recall the circling methods taught in Phase 5. Get him to circle at several different distances from you. If he cannot find it, back up toward the last place he was definitely tracking (which is probably near the corner). If he can still not find it there, and particularly if there is some unusual scent condition in the area, circle your dog in ever-larger circles until he can reach past the unusual scent condition. Let your dog lead if you can, but don't be afraid of doing a little leading yourself if the dog is about to quit. If your dog has been tracking well up to this point, the judges may cut you a little slack about guiding your dog since they will probably recognize the scenting difficulty. However, even if they fail you for guiding, you will be no worse off than if they fail you for quitting. I believe it is no worse to be failed for guiding than it is to be failed for quitting.

Do use your corner communication sequence on every corner in the test. It will help you and your dog maintain confidence in each other and will significantly improve your performance on the test.

Tracking is a wonderful sport. If you have had a great time training for your TD, you may want to go on to train for the TDX and VST tests. These tests are much more difficult than the TD, but your TD training has laid the solid foundation upon which your advanced training will be laid.

Part II – Advanced Tracking Toward the TDX Test

TDX is a complex, strenuous team sport. There are a number of advanced skills that a dog and handler should master in preparation for a TDX test. This training plan combined with your thoughtful application of the ideas presented here, some perseverance and hard work, and enjoying the training process will prepare you and your dog for one of the most challenging and rewarding tests in dogdom.

You will find this TDX material is presented in a more terse fashion than the TD material in Part I. This is due, in part, to the nature of good TDX training that demands adapting each track design to the particular dog and his current strengths and weaknesses. For this reason, Phases A and B show training schedules but not sample training maps for each session. The terseness is also due to the need, in Phases C and D, to adapt both the training schedule and the individual track designs to variation in each dog's current skills and learning style. For these reasons, Part II describes the training structure you will need to successfully train for the TDX and leaves the elaboration of the structure to you, the trainer. Given the foundation developed in the first part of the book, and it is wise to review that foundation from time to time, you can be confident that your thoughtful elaboration will be successful.

Training Philosophy:

In a TDX test, the dog faces a variety of complex tracking problems. If we practiced and proofed them all, the dog would lose motivation to track and probably die of old age before being ready to enter a test. Rather than proof all possible TDX tracking problems, we expose the dog and handler to a representative sample of TDX problems, we teach the dog to solve complex tracking problems, and we maintain such a high level of motivation that the dog is willing and anxious to solve them.

Not all good TD dog-handler teams will be successful in advanced tracking. Most excellent and very good TD teams can succeed with the TDX, but those teams that just squeaked by their TD may find the TDX more difficult than they care to attempt. If you are in doubt, start and see how you and your dog respond to the necessary training. By the middle of Phase C, you will either find yourself totally committed or you will have realized that there are more important things to do with this particular dog.

TDX Test Overview:

A TDX test track should conform to the following guidelines:

- Age: 3-5 hours old
- Length: 800-1000 yards
- Start: single flag start
- Articles: four, one at the start, two intermediate, plus the final one
- Corners: 5-7 corners (at least 3 must be 90°, some out in the open)
- Crosstracks: 2 laid about 90 minutes after the main track
- Obstacles: at least 2 difficult obstacles or compound obstacles.

TDX Training Overview:

- First, gradually age the track to three hours while introducing the dog to single flag starts, multiple articles, and simple obstacles.
- Second, return to fresh tracks but with crosstracks at half the age of the track and gradually age the track to five hours.
- Third, vary age between two and five hours while introducing more simple obstacles as well as complex compound obstacles.
- Once the dog is extremely happy tracking five-hour-old tracks, handles crosstracks, all simple obstacles, and most compound obstacles with confidence and without help, test the dog on a blind TDX-like track laid by a trusted tracklayer.
- Once the dog and handler can pass more than one-third of their blind TDX test-like tracks, they start to enter tests while working on improving their problem areas.
- When they get into a test, follow the performance peaking procedure described in phase 8 above.

Important: Throughout TDX training, frequently intersperse the main training sessions with **motivational tracks** – tracks that are much younger and much easier than the main training tracks. In addition, throughout TDX training, **condition yourself and your dog** by long walks or jogs in hilly backcountry. Always keep a **training journal** so you can look back and discover what types of conditions you have missed in your recent training and so you can detect how new problem behavior began.

Basics Skills Revisited

Maintain the fundamental principles presented in Part I:
- Motivation, motivation, motivation.
- The dog should track very close to the track.
- The dog is responsible for leading you down the track.
- You must maintain a light firm tension on the line at all times; stay in contact with your dog.
- Corner communications!!!
- Read your dog.
- Read the landscape – maintain your orientation in the field.
- Organize your dog's search when he has trouble.
- When your dog needs help, do so happily! It is an opportunity to teach.

As the track gets older and older, many dogs that stayed close to the track start to act like the scent is "too strong" or "bad smelling" right on the track and these dogs seem to prefer to track several feet downwind of the track. Don't let them hoodwink you. Use line tension and raising your hand to make it easiest for the dog to stay right on the track. You will have a much easier job reading your dog as a result.

Corner communication takes on added importance in TDX work and takes on the added dimension of obstacle communication as well. Your dog will face situations in this work where there is a sequence of closely spaced obstacles. If your dog can clearly communicate to you that he is on the track in only a short distance and if you can quickly communicate to him your confidence that he is right, you will both be fully prepared for the next obstacle. If there is doubt in your mind when he reaches that next obstacle, both of you will have difficulty overcoming the obstacle.

Advanced Basics

When a track has multiple articles, the **intermediate articles** are great places to reward your dog and to give him water. Your dog should become so enthusiastic about the track that unless you make finding articles very special, your dog may overrun articles without being bothered to point them out to you. So you will need to build both a very strong tracking drive as well as a very strong article indication. Great treats, toys in the articles, fun play at each article, and genuine enthusiasm on your part, combined with never allowing him to miss an article, will build that strong article indication. Play the glove game at the end of the track and on non-tracking days.

Dogs may be taught to **indicate articles** in a variety of ways. Some people advocate having their dog retrieve the article, but I advocate having them down or sit at the article. The reason I do this is because it makes for more reliable restarts. Should you and your dog be tracking several feet downwind of the track and the dog curves in to the article and retrieves it to you, you and the dog will end up a few feet off the track when you restart him. You might be restarting him on a deer track for all you know. On the other hand, if your dog downs at the article and you walk up to the dog, then when you restart him, you will be restarting him right on the track. How fortuitous!

To **restart** your dog after playing with him at the intermediate article, just stand up and give your tracking command. Most dogs will quickly realize that there is more tracking to do and go right back to work. Any time a dog has trouble restarting, happily help him find the track.

TDX dogs must be able to determine **track direction**. Throughout your training, you have avoided letting your dog backtrack tracks. Whenever the opportunity arises during circling or searching, keep him from backtracking a track more than about 6-15 feet. Most dogs will learn to determine track direction within 2-5 footsteps and many can determine the direction within a single footprint. I speculate that the 2-5 footstep dogs learn to distinguish very subtle scent strength differences, while the single-footprint dogs learn to distinguish the smell of the heavy heel compression from the relatively lighter toe push-off or that the heel somehow smells different than the toe. I prefer the single-footstep dog, so I gradually limit the backtracking distance as the dog gains track direction skill.

Once a track gets to be an hour and a half old, **food drops** tend to get dry, covered with ants, or stolen by birds. So I tend to use frequent articles along the track that give me the opportunity to reward my dog with food. I will also use cupcakes which are a small piece of food frozen within a cupcake paper full of water. Placed upside-down on the track, by the time the dog gets the cupcake, the ice is melted and the food is still fresh. You may also use jackpots that are food in small margarine or yogurt tubs and that are left on the track sealed. You may have to open the lid for the dog once he finds it. Dogs clicker trained can be signaled while they are tracking with a click. Verbal praise is also good if used sparingly.

TDX training takes a long time, most of which will be spent in phase C. It is normal to **take a break** one or more times during this training because the weather is too hot, the snow too deep, or for some other reason. Resuming training correctly can quickly bring you and your dog back to the skill level where you stopped while restoring even more enthusiasm in the dog. Resuming training incorrectly can solidify your problem areas and seriously damage motivation.

Short breaks of a couple of weeks can be ignored while breaks of two months or more cause a significant drop in proficiency and must be handled carefully. Depending on your dog, breaks of 3 weeks to 7 weeks may be more or less significant.

Resume training by starting with a 45-minute-old track and adding 30 minutes to each track until you get back to the oldest track you had done before. If you completed much of phase B, have crosstracks on at least two of these tracks. If it has been a really long time since you last tracked with this dog, start with a 20-minute-old track. Then resume your training on the session two before the last one completed before the break. If you try to speed up your training progress by skipping this resuming-after-a-break sequence, you will actually slow it down with many additional problem-solving and motivation building sessions.

A typical resuming-after-a-break sequence for a dog whose last track prior to the break was session B.7.

Session	Track Age	Crosstrack Age	Crosstrack Flags	Track Length	Number Corners	Number Obstacles
R.1	:45	none		400-500	4-5	0
R.2	1:15	none		500-600	4-5	1
R.3	1:45	:50	On track	600-700	4-5	1
R.4	:45	none		400	3-5	0
R.5	2:15	1:00	5 yds off	500-600	4-5	0
R.6	2:40	None		600-700	4-5	1

Then return to session B.5 and continue on from there.

The figure below shows some typical articles and equipment for TDX training. Clockwise from the upper left is a scarf, some yarn and a clothes pin for marking tracks, a colorful plastic paper clip, a sock, a wallet, a small flag, a glove, an eye glass case, a roll of surveyors tape, and a belt.

Phase A. Aging the Track to Three Hours.

Strategy:

- Gradually age the track to three hours old.
- Introduce the dog to single flag starts.
- Introduce the dog to simple obstacles.
- Introduce the dog to multiple articles.

Schedule:

Session	Track Age	Track Length	Number Corners	Number Obstacles	Number Articles	Start Angle
A.1	1:00	400-500	3-4	0	2	0° _
A.2	1:10	500-600	4-5	1	3	15° L
A.3	1:20	500-600	4-5	1	3	15° R
A.4	1:30	500-600	4-5	1	3	15° ?
A.5	:45	400	3-5	0	2	30° L
A.6	1:40	600-700	4-5	0	3	30° R
A.7	1:50	600-700	5-6	1	3	30° ?
A.8	2:00	600-700	5-6	1	4	45° L
A.9	:30	500	3-5	0	3	45° R
A.10	2:10	600-700	4-5	1	3	45° ?
A.11	2:20	700-800	5-7	1	4	60° L
A.12	2:30	700-800	5-7	1	4	60° R
A.13	45	400	3-5	0	3	75° L
A.14	2:45	600-800	5-7	1	5	75° R
A.15	3:00	600-800	5-7	1	5	90° L
A.16	3:15	600-800	5-7	1	5	90° R
A.17	1:00	600	4-6	0	4	any
A.18	1:30	1000	6-8	0	6	any
A.19	:45	400	2-4	0	3	any
A.20	review					

Discussion:

All tracks should have a single flag start with an article at the flag. Approach the flag with the dog at the angle indicated. Down your dog right at the article – do not let him start up without spending half a minute to several minutes at the start. Let him play with the article if you can keep his nose right over the start.

The first track has two articles, one at the start and one at the end. The other tracks have one or more intermediate articles in addition to the start and end article. Use a glove or wallet at the end. Use scarves, socks, plastic eyeglass cases, belts, hats, combs, and other personal articles for the other locations. When you introduce a new article, particularly one of plastic or metal, put it first at the start. On a subsequent track, use it as an intermediate article, but put it in an open location where you can be sure the dog will find it. Mark the location with a flag 20 feet before the article so you will know exactly where it is located. If he ignores it, restrain him and make a big fuss about how much fun it is to find this article just like he did it himself.

You will find it convenient to be able to mark important areas of the track in subtler ways than a big old stake. Many people use orange clothes pins clipped on nearby branches or they use brightly colored yarn or surveyor's tape. Placing them up high seems to allow them to avoid notice by most dogs.

Only use simple obstacles in this phase. Be sure you know where the track goes through the obstacle and be ready to happily help the dog through. Use dirt road crossings, barb wire fences, changes in cover, trees, streams and gullies. Avoid multiple obstacles close together. Make a track shorter than normal rather than make it too difficult.

Your dog will have difficulty with track age once or twice during this phase. He may quit, act like the track is very difficult to find, or track very slowly with little commitment. This is normal. You must be prepared to help your dog through a track until he gains confidence in handling these more difficult scenting conditions. You may want to put a flag midway down each leg so you can keep your bearings when you need to help your dog.

Whenever the dog really loses the track, you first remind him what he is following by having him sniff the start article. This will be a valuable technique to use in a test should your dog lose the track or get confused. So whenever you need to help the dog (except on crosstracks that are introduced in phase B), first show him the start article and have him get a good sniff of it. Then ask him to track again. If he still has trouble, you will start to actively help him. Remember to put on a dynamic outward display of enthusiasm whenever you help him. Show the dog how much fun it is and how much confidence you have in him. Go right up beside your dog, hold the line right above the harness, tickle the grass on the track in front of the dog. Step forward with the dog and tickle some more. Keep doing that until the dog takes off in front of you and starts tracking again. Be sure you are having fun and be sure the dog knows it!

I lay almost all my own TDX training tracks because I always want to know exactly where the track is located in case I have to help my dog. Once I have the dog trained, I introduce other tracklayers so the dog is familiar with other footsteps and I am familiar with handling this dog on blind tracks. If this is your first time training for a TDX, you will need to work quite a few blind tracks in phase C and D to become proficient handling a dog through blind tracks.

If you have already trained your dog on 2-hour-old tracks, you may wonder if you can skip right to session 1.10. Unless you incorporated single flag angle starts, multiple articles, and obstacles in your previous training, you need to complete this whole phase. Even so, repeat this material if you took a break for more than 2 months or if the dog is not highly motivated as described in Phase 7.

Keep in mind the discussion in Basics Skills Revisited on page 136 and Advanced Basics on page 137 throughout your training.

A sample track taken from Mr. Q's tracking journal (session A.8) is shown on the next page. It shows the type of information I kept in his tracking log. I use index cards and write the notes of the back of the card. Many people use larger sheets, but I find index card convenient because they fit in my pocket.

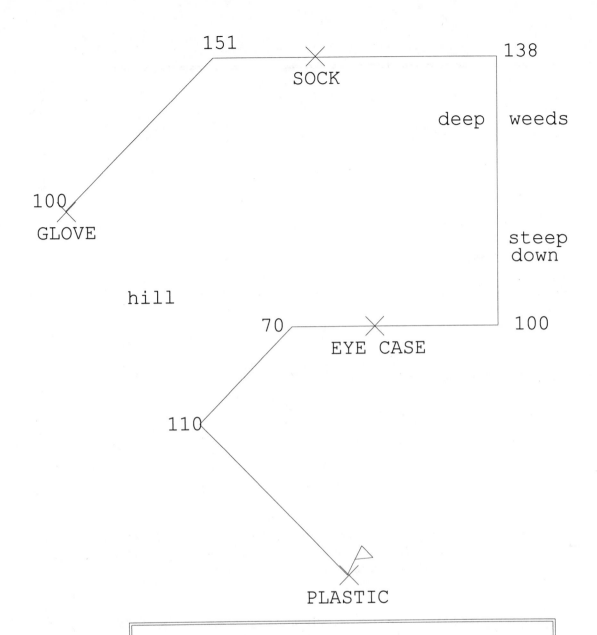

151   ✕   138

SOCK

deep | weeds

100 ✕

GLOVE

steep
down

hill

70   ✕   100

EYE CASE

110 ✕

✕

PLASTIC

```
DOG: MR. Q
LAYER: SIL
FIELD: GATEHOUSE/VALE
AGE:   2:00    LENGTH: 669
DATE:
WEATHER: STORMY, HEAVY RAIN
WIND:    GUSTY TO 50 MPH
REPORT: excellent.
good start, art. recog.
Not bothered by wind.
some tiring at 450, but willing
```

Reminder

These issues are repeated here because they are so important to successful advanced training.

- **Motivational Tracks:** Frequently intersperse the main training sessions with motivational tracks – tracks that are much younger and much easier than the main training tracks.

- **Conditioning:** condition yourself and your dog by long walks or jogs in hilly backcountry.

- **Corner Communication:**
  - ❖ Your dog clearly indicates loss of track within a few yards of the actual corner.
  - ❖ You read your dog's behavior, recognize the loss of track and stop.
  - ❖ Your dog purposefully searches for the new leg while you maintain a light comfortable tension with no slack. Your dog notices the new leg as he is searching and follows it in a straight line a few feet.
  - ❖ You increase the tension slightly and verbally ask the dog "Is this the good track?"
  - ❖ Your dog leans into the harness.
  - ❖ You *immediately* decrease the tension back to your normal light-comfortable tension, step out behind the dog, and praise your dog quietly.
  - ❖ Your dog receives a reward a short distance down the new leg

- **Journal:** Always keep a training journal so you can look back and discover what types of conditions you have missed in your recent training and so you can detect how new problem behavior began.

- **Close to the Track:** The dog should track very close to the track. Right over the footprints is ideal, a few feet off is OK, but we use increased tension to make it slightly harder for the dog to track there, and we stop the dog if they try to track more than six feet away from the track.

- **Active Handling:** Read your dog, read the landscape, organize his search, trust your dog.

- **Helping:** When your dog needs help, do so happily! It is an opportunity to teach.

Phase B. Crosstracks.

Strategy:

- Gradually age the main track to five hours old.
- Introduce the dog to crosstracks.
- Introduce more simple obstacles.

Schedule:

Session	Track Age	Crosstrack Age	Crosstrack Flags	Track Length	Number Corners	Number Obstacles
B.1	1:00	:30	On track	400-500	4-5	0
B.2	1:20	:40	On track	500-600	4-5	1
B.3	1:40	:50	On track	600-700	4-5	1
B.4	:45	none		400	3-5	0
B.5	2:00	1:00	5 yds off	600-700	4-5	1
B.6	2:20	1:10	5 yds off	500-600	5-6	1
B.7	2:40	1:20	5 yds off	500-600	5-6	1
B.8	:30	none		500	3-5	0
B.9	3:00	1:30	10 yds off	600-700	5-7	1
B.10	3:20	1:40	10 yds off	500-600	5-7	1
B.11	3:40	1:50	10 yds off	500-600	5-7	1
B.12	:45	none		400	3-5	0
B.13	4:00	1:15	15 yds off	600-800	5-7	1
B.14	4:20	1:30	15 yds off	600-700	5-7	1
B.15	4:40	1:45	15 yds off	500-600	5-7	1
B.16	1:00	none		600	4-6	0
B.17	5:00	1:30	15 yds off	400	4-5	0
B.18	:45	none		400	2-4	0
B.19	review					

Discussion:

Crosstracks are very important in TDX because they are the only type of "obstacle" you know will be on every test track. This phase may seem slightly long, but you are really accomplishing several goals in addition to learning crosstracks. This second gradual increase of track age is critical in building the dog's confidence and skill in handling old tracks. And the additional obstacle work will build an important foundation for the phase C work to follow. Even if you have worked extensively on fields with natural foot traffic, explicitly teaching crosstracks is important.

All tracks should have a single flag start with an article at the flag. Approach the flag with the dog at a random angle between plus and minus 90°. Remember to down your dog right at the article; do not let him start up without spending half a minute to several minutes at the start. Let him play with the article if you can keep his nose right over the start. If your dog is not committing to the track quickly at the start, precede each main track with a 50 yard starter track laid right after the main track but run right before the main track.

These tracks should all have four or more articles. I use articles wherever I want to reward my dog. He gets lots to goodies when he finds an article, so he is rewarded for "overcoming" the tracking problems and for finding the article. It tends to make him article sure and keeps him motivated. Every once in a while, "forget" to give him treats after an article so he is accustomed to restarting without a reward. See page 137 for more ideas for rewarding your dog on the track.

Before you start crosstracks, you must decide whether you are going to allow the tracklayer to cross their own track. We did this for many years because the dogs could learn to distinguish track age and stay with the same age track on which they started. It is very convenient to lay your own crosstracks since you never have to worry about getting another person or two to lay them at just the right time. However, it may have a big disadvantage in the age of VST since VST requires a dog to follow the starting tracklayer rather than the starting track age. By teaching a dog to attend to track age and not tracklayer identity on TDX crosstracks, you are teaching him the wrong lesson for VST. Therefore, I now recommend you always use crosstrack layers who are different from your tracklayer. If you are sure you do not want this dog to do VST, go ahead and cross your own track. It works very well as a TDX-only training technique.

In AKC tests, crosstracks are made by two people walking side-by-side about four feet apart. In CKC, crosstracks are made by a single person. It is common to be unable to have access to crosstrack layers every time you can track. On those days that even a single crosstrack layer is available, lay the next track in sequence from this phase. A single person can walk the crosstrack twice, either up-and-back putting down two crosstracks that go in different directions, or twice in the same direction. I prefer the twice in the same direction, but use the up and back method when that is all I can get the crosstrack layer to do. On tracking days when no crosstrack layer is present, lay a track from phase C.

As the tracklayer lays the track, place tall visible flags each place the crosstrackers should cross the track. Make sure the crosstrack flags are different than other flags you use to mark the track. Note on the track-layer map the crosstrack landmark in the direction the crosstrack layers will be walking. It is very important to be extra-extra careful about the crosstracks because crosstrack layers have been known to go astray when given sloppy or inadequate directions.

Crosstracks in tests should always cross the main track at 90°. In training, 30% to 50% of the crosstracks should be at angles down to 45°. Angled crosstracks solidifies the dog's understanding of crosstracks.

Crosstrack age refers to the time between when the tracklayer lays the track and when the crosstrack layers lay the crosstracks. Crosstrack layers should always stay away from the area of the start. Keeping at least 75 yards from the start is a good idea.

After the first few crosstrack sessions, the crosstrack layers move the crosstrack flags a few yards off the track. Once this happens, the handler will have to remember that the flags are no longer directly on the main track. Moving the flags keeps the dog from becoming dependent on the crosstrack flags as a signal that these are crosstracks. The distance to move them depends on the dog's tendency to notice flags, but they should remain in the general area to remind the handler that this is a crosstrack and not a corner.

Note that the main tracks are not extremely long. Avoid long tracks while introducing new material but some crosstrack designs require a fair amount of yardage. Several typical crosstrack designs are reproduced on the following pages. The first design is an M-shape crosstrack over a long straight leg and can be seen in the first track diagram below. You need a long field to accomplish this design. Another pattern is called a "hat over a hat" or a "U over a C" which can be seen in the second figure below. Both designs create four crosstracks on a track. A third design has a straight crosstrack over multiple legs of a zigzag or S-shaped track. This can be called the dollar sign $ design and can be used to cross the track several times depending on the number of zigs and zags that make up the main track. Whatever your design, keep the crosstrack layers 75 yards from the start and 50 yards from other parts of the main track.

Handling on the crosstrack is important. Until the dog learns the concept of distinguishing the crosstracks from the main track, he is likely to take the fresher crosstracks any time he notices them. Therefore, your job is to teach the dog that the articles, fun, and goodies are found on the main track, not on the crosstracks. You do this by allowing the dog to investigate the crosstracks anytime he notices them; let him follow the crosstracks 20-40 feet while using higher than normal tension. If he does not break off on his own, move forward on the main track until you are a few yards past the crosstracks while calling happily to the dog about how exciting and cool the track is over here! You must be happy and enthusiastic. You are teaching, not correcting. Lean down and tickle the grass right on the track as you reel in the dog to you, show him the track and help him down the main track until he takes off in front of you. It is a good lesson anytime you are able to show the dog like this. He will learn.

As the dog learns about crosstracks and starts to reject most of the crosstracks he notices, you allow him less distance up the crosstrack before calling him to the main track. Even after your dog is very experienced with crosstracks, occasionally he will be fooled by a particular set of tantalizing crosstrack conditions. Maintain a happy and enthusiastic attitude! It is an opportunity to remind the dog to stay on the main track.

A typical crosstrack map from my own tracking journal is reproduced below. Note that the three obstacles (steep up and two road crossings) are more than the desired number of one for track 2.5. This particular dog had already handled these obstacles before, so it was OK for him. Note also that there should have been articles 30-40 yards past each crosstrack, which means that there must be 60-80 yards between crosstracks. The next two crosstrack diagrams are idealized and should be adjusted to fit the field conditions available.

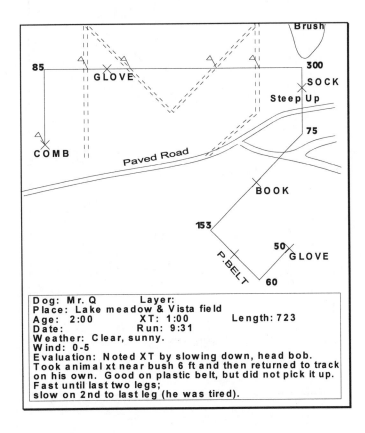

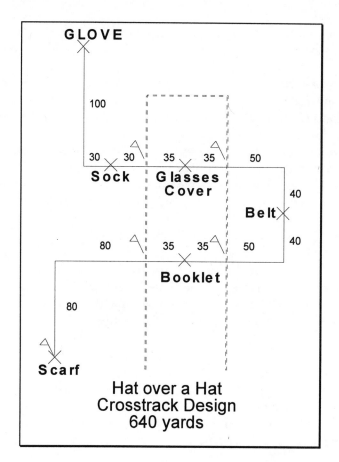

GLOVE

100

30 30 **Sock** 35 35 **Glasses Cover** 50

40

Belt

40

80 35 35 50

Booklet

80

Scarf

Hat over a Hat
Crosstrack Design
640 yards

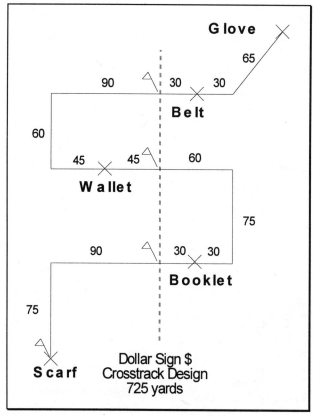

Glove

65

90 30 30

Belt

60

45 **Wallet** 45 60

75

90 30 30

Booklet

75

Scarf

Dollar Sign $
Crosstrack Design
725 yards

Phase C. Skill Improvement.

Strategy:

- Build skill fluency in dog and handler.
- Vary age between two and five hours.
- Introduce additional simple obstacles and introduce complex compound obstacles.

Schedule:

There is no fixed schedule for this phase. Plan to track 2-3 times a week at most. For AKC, expect to spend 4 to 24 months in this phase; that means 50 to 200 sessions over whatever period of time it takes to met the criteria described in the next phase. For CKC only, you will not have to prepare for compound obstacles, complex obstacles, or particularly difficult obstacles. So the time needed for CKC skill development should be considerably less than that required for AKC. For either AKC or CKC, if ever there was a time where haste makes waste, it is now. Don't rush. Have fun. The title will come if you allow you and your dog the chance to perfect your skills.

Make sure every third or fourth session is a motivational track. If you start to lose motivation, alternate training tracks with motivational tracks. If your dog's motivation is good, introduce new obstacles on a motivational track while keeping the rest of the track very simple! A sample sequence might look something like:

Session	Strategic Focus	Track Age	Crosstrack Age	Track Length	Number Corners	Number Obstacles
C.i	Complexity	3:00	1:30	600-800	6-7	3
C.j	Hard obstacle	4:30	none	500-600	4-5	1
C.k	New obstacle	3:30	none	600-700	4-5	2
C.l	Motivation	1:00	none	400-500	3-4	1
C.m	Age & obstacles	4:00	1:45	500-700	4-5	2
C.n	Hard obstacle	3:30	none	500-600	4-5	2
C.o	Age	5:00	none	600-800	5-6	1
C.p	length	:45	none	1000-1100	6-7	0
C.q	Motivation	1:00	none	300-400	2-3	0

Discussion:

This should be the longest phase of your TDX training. Unfortunately, many handlers get so excited that their dog can handle some advanced skills that they start entering tests now. A very few lucky dogs and handlers pass in such circumstances, but the vast majority of them fail. Due to the two to four weeks spent peaking performance before each test and the depression that naturally follows each failure, such handlers waste a lot of time and many never really get ready.

Other handlers notice that the TDX tests in their area have many more entrants than tracks, so they decide to enter the test lottery before they are ready, or take long breaks between their training and then try to cram right before a test that they are lucky enough to get into. This is another big waste of time for the same reason as described above.

A better strategy is to volunteer to lay tracks or crosstracks at tests in your area or to spectate at tests in your area. You will learn about the terrain and type of obstacles used at local tests as well as gain a better overall understanding of the complexity level of the test. Spending a weekend or three during phase C laying track at local tests will prepare you better for the test than entering a test.

TDX tests are fundamentally difficult. ***Your quickest way to pass is to be fully prepared before focusing on entering tests.*** Even once you are fully prepared, your chance of passing is less than 50%. I start entering tests when I think my dog has a 33% chance of passing a test as demonstrated by his successfully passing all aspects of at least one out of three test-like blind tracks. At the very least, wait until you can pass all aspects of at least one test-like blind track, even if it takes you more than three tries to pass that one. For your reference, the AKC pass rate is about 15%.

The purpose of this phase is to improve you and your dog's skills. The purpose of the next phase is to practice test-like blind tracks. You need to design tracks to introduce, teach and proof many different issues. The following tables help you understand and monitor the sort of issues that occur in advanced training and TDX tests. To design your tracks, use the tables along with the considerations described below in "Monitoring and controlling track difficulty" on page 151.

Keep in mind the discussion in Basics Skills Revisited on page 136 and Advanced Basics on page 137 throughout your training. In particular, incorporate the three indispensable training techniques: intersperse motivational tracks, condition yourself and the dog, and keep a tracking journal.

Obstacles and Ground Covers

Many trainers do not consider all the types of ground covers and obstacles they and their dog might face in a test. You should be familiar with all common ones used in tests in your area as well as a representative sample of others. Remember that you are not trying to handle all possible obstacles you might encounter in any test. That endeavor will wear you and your dog out.

When introducing a new type of ground cover or a new type of obstacle, try to do so in a controlled fashion. This is particularly true of difficult covers and obstacles. Try to design the track so there is some easy tracking right before the difficult area, some easy tracking right after the difficult area, and an article 20-40 yards past the difficult area where you can reward your dog for a job well done.

The following tables list many types of covers and obstacles. The tables are in a form that you can monitor the number of times your dog has recently experienced these covers and obstacles and rate their recent performance in these covers and obstacles. Periodically fill in these tables. You will notice situations that need additional work.

If you are interested in the AKC VST test, now is a good time to introduce some elements of that test if you have not already done so. Most VST/TDX people seem to work on these tests in sequence rather than in parallel, but you can use some VST elements to solidify your dog's understanding of TDX tracking. VST uses urban/suburban settings such as community college campuses or industrial parks where there is a mix of lawns, sidewalks, buildings, and parking lots. Expect your dog to track over lawns where many other people are walking, along concrete walkways, around buildings, through breezeways, and across blacktop roads and parking lots. Expect this to be a very different tracking experience for your dog than what he is used to in the meadow and woods, so introduce him to it carefully in a step-by-step fashion. In particular, expect blacktop to be a very difficult surface and expect buildings to be difficult obstacles. *Aside: this paragraph does not purport to tell you how to train for the VST test, just how to use VST elements to solidify your dog's understanding of advanced tracking.*

Ground Covers and Obstacles

Ground Covers:	Num.	Rate	Num.	Rate	Num.	Rate	Num.	Rate
Grass	Tall		Medium		Short		Lawn	
Grass	Grazed		Swamp		Marsh		Manured	
Weeds	Thistle		Pampas		Nettles		Other	
Covers under Trees	Pine-Fir		Cypress-Cedar		Oak		Deciduous	
Dirt	Plowed		Hard Packed		Animal Pens		Furrowed	
Unusual	Gravel		Sand		Burnt		Freshly Mowed	
Crops	Corn -Tall		Corn Stubble		Vegetable		Other	

Obstacles:	Cross or Thru		Turn On or In		Turn Into		Zigzag Thru	
	Num.	Rate	Num.	Rate	Num.	Rate	Num.	Rate
Dirt Road								
Paved Road								
Tree Line								
Brush Line								
Hedge								
Stump								
Fallen Tree								
Rocks								
Foot Bridge								
Derelict – Ruin – Abandoned Car								
Irrigation Ditch								
Stream								
Dry Gulch								
Standing Water								

Obstacles:	Num.	Rate	Num.	Rate	Num.	Rate	Num.	Rate
Animals	Ground		Horses		Cows		Birds	
Fences	Barbed Wire		Climbing		Fallen Down		Turn At	
Corners	Acute		Curved		Sweeping		False	
Tall Changes in Elevation	Tree Line		Wall		Cliff Above		Cliff Below	
Footpaths	Cross		Follow		Turn on		Turn off	
Curved Legs or Serpentine Legs	Sharp		Wide					

Track age and other considerations

These tables as well as the ones above can help you monitor your recent tracking activity.

Track Age (Hours):	1-2	2-3	3-4	4-5	5+
Number of Tracks within last few months.					
Rate Recent Accuracy					
Rate Recent Enthusiasm					

Length (yards):	Up to 400	400-600	600-800	800-1000	1000+
Number of Tracks within last few months.					
Rate Recent Accuracy					
Rate Recent Enthusiasm					

Starts (Hours):	1-2	2-3	3-4	4-5	5+
Rate Recent Accuracy					
Rate Recent Enthusiasm					

Corners:	90° in Open	Acute	Near Obstacle	In Obstacle	Curved
Number of Tracks within last few months.					
Rate Recent Accuracy					
Rate Recent Enthusiasm					

Crosstracks (minutes):	Up to 60	60-75	75-90	90-105	105+
Number of Tracks within last few months.					
Rate Recent Accuracy					
Rate Recent Enthusiasm					

Articles:	Leather	Cloth	Sock	Belt	Paper
Number of Articles within last few months.					
Rate Recent Accuracy					
Rate Recent Enthusiasm					
Articles:	Soft Plastic	Hard Plastic	Metal	Heavily Scented	Lightly Scented
Number of Articles within last few months.					
Rate Recent Accuracy					
Rate Recent Enthusiasm					

Restarts After Articles:	Leather	Cloth	Other	With Reward	Without Reward
Rate Recent Enthusiasm when Restarting					

Compound Obstacles.

Although AKC has minimum distances between crosstracks, articles and obstacles, there is no minimum distance between a corner and an obstacle or between two obstacles. The simpler the rest of your test, the more likely it is that the judges will use compound obstacles or a corner before, in or after an obstacle. You must be prepared for compound obstacles.

Once a dog is comfortable handling most typical obstacles found in tests in your area, start to introduce him to compound obstacles and corners in, before or after obstacles. Keep these compound obstacles well separated from other problem areas, and put an article 30-50 yards past the area so the dog can be rewarded for completing the compound obstacle. Help the dog if you need to. This is another step in your dog's learning and it is an important step.

Typical compound obstacles are:
- corners in heavy weeds, under trees, on dirt or an unusual cover;
- corners on or before or after a road, tree line, fallen tree, foot bridge, ditch, stream, footpath;
- complexes of obstacles such as the junction of a stream and a footpath, two roads;
- sequences of obstacles in close proximity such as a fence-ditch-road-ditch-fence sequence.

You may notice your dog quitting at difficult compound obstacles – it is as if they are saying, "This is too difficult." Use it as a opportunity to encourage your dog to go on. Be happy and show your enthusiasm for the track and how much fun it is to be on the track with your dog. Expect your dog to learn that difficult obstacles are a part of the activity and that if they keep searching, they will find it, the track will become easy again, and they will have a lot of fun. As you are working difficult obstacles, pay particular attention to monitoring and limiting the overall difficulty of the tracks as described below.

Monitoring and controlling track difficulty.

Monitoring and controlling track difficulty is the art and science of the successful tracking trainer. It is very important and needs to be done carefully and thoughtfully. Intuition helps as well.

I have developed several mathematical schemes to calculate the difficulty of tracks as well as to rate the success the dog is having on the track. None of the schemes is successful enough to repeat in detail here. The schemes try to combine track age, length, number of corners, obstacles, crosstracks, and articles as measured against the experience level of the dog. The schemes all end up adding apple obstacles to orange obstacles and producing a lemon of a result.

However, to be a successful trainer, you need to control the overall difficulty of the tracks you lay or have laid for your dog. A dog that faces too many consecutive tracks that are too difficult for him will lose motivation. The dog will learn to expect failure and will learn to expect you to help him find the track. This does not make for a passing performance in a blind test track.

On the other hand, a dog that only faces simple tracks will not be well prepared for the test. So a trainer must use the best gauge and the only reliable gauge for track difficulty that he or she has available. That finely crafted precision instrument is, of course, your dog. At the end of every track, once you are done playing with your dog and are back at base camp, take a few minutes to recall the dog's performance and give it an overall rating. I use Excellent, Very Good, Good, Needs-Work, Flawed. Use any scale you like. Try to be objective in your ratings; you are rating the overall performance of the track designer, the tracklayer, the dog and the handler, not just the dog itself. Talk it over with a tracking friend.

Base your tracking plans on the following general rules:

- If you have a long sequence of excellent ratings, you need to up the difficulty of the tracks. Once you have raised it to test-like conditions, you are ready to move on to the next phase. I also look for several key indicators before trying the next phase: a dog that is enthusiastic when tracking a four-hour-old track on a warm day, a dog that rejects crosstracks whenever he notices them, and a dog that can solve most new complex compound obstacles that he faces.
- Most training should have a mixture of excellent, very good, and good ratings with a very occasional needs-work or flawed rating. This type of training challenges the dog and gives him a fair opportunity to learn new skills. The optimal mix depends on your dog's enjoyment of being challenged. Whatever you do, keep the ratings mix high enough to maintain enthusiasm.
- When too many training sessions have low ratings, something is wrong and should be fixed. Perhaps you are challenging your dog too quickly. Perhaps you have too many obstacles on the track for the current skill of your dog. Perhaps your dog has lost motivation for some reason, and you need to rebuild his tracking drive. Perhaps you have been mishandling the dog and created confusion for the dog. Don't blame your dog; don't blame yourself; these things happen and good trainers find a way out of them. Whatever the reason, it is up to you to find it and do whatever is necessary to remedy the problem.

Review phase 7 for ideas on critically evaluating your dog and creating remediation plans to correct the shortcomings. The four questions with minor adjustment still apply:

- When you arrive at the tracking field, is your dog obviously excited to be there?
- In the last five tracks, did you help him find the track more than twice?
- On the best 80% of his opportunities to work a corner/cover change/obstacle/crosstrack, does he find and commit to the leg quickly and enthusiastically?
- On blind tracks, do you read your dog's tracking behavior on corners/cover changes/obstacles/ crosstracks and believe your dog quickly and confidently?

Focus on one training shortcoming at a time. Design tracks that address the chosen shortcoming within an overall track layout that assures a high level of success. Focus on the chosen shortcoming for several sessions; as you and the dog master the area of focus, shift your focus onto the next training shortcoming. Periodically, review previously mastered shortcomings to solidify mastery. Within a relatively short time, you and your dog will improve tremendously and be ready for the next phase.

Some Problem Solving Techniques

- **Weak or no article indication**: Place a marker 20 feet before every article, don't let dog pass the article, lots of praise and reward for stopping or being stopped.
- **Backtracking:** Lay 3-5 straight 75-100 yard tracks with flags at each end and with only an end article. Approach track from the side at 90° about 30 yards from start. Let dog backtrack a maximum of 15'. Reduce the maximum backtrack distance over multiple sessions.
- **Takes crosstracks:** Repeat Phase B with marked crosstracks. Pay particular attention to the way you call the dog from crosstrack over to the main track.
- **Distracted by ground animals or birds:** Lay tracks that cross areas with ground animals or birds. Lead up to this area with easy tracking. Have an article 30 yards past area. Let dog investigate area briefly, then ask to return to the main track. Help him happily, if you need to help. Reward dog with a jackpot (something the dog really wants) at the next article. Repeat for many sessions, but limit distraction area to once per track. If dog refuses to leave distraction, tell him "NO!", then be happy.
- **Poor starts:** Lay a 50-75 yard straight starter track after laying every track, but run starter before main track. Put an article 30-100 yards after each main track start. Fun at the end every track.
- **Other**: Also review and adapt the problem solving discussion on page 114 to TDX conditions.

Phase D. Test-like Blind Tracks.

Strategy:

- Test the dog and handler to see if they are ready to enter tests.
- Provide practice for the handler in reading his dog.
- Provide practice for the dog in leading his handler along a blind track.

Schedule:

Again, there is no formal schedule for this phase. The general idea is to get a trusted tracking friend to lay a test-like blind track for your dog and have two other people lay your crosstracks. Sounds like a tracking party to me. Bring muffins!

Schedule these test-like blind tracks no more frequently than once every two to six weeks. You need time between tests to work on what you learned from the last test. In between test-like tracks, design tracks that contain specific situations that will challenge your dog in a way he needs to be challenged. Surround this challenging area by easy tracking segments, and always follow a difficult problem area with an article so you can reward your dog with lots of goodies.

Another good thing to do between test-like tracks is to proof unusual test-like conditions. Track in the same field two days in a row and crisscross yesterday's track. This is described in more detail in Phase 8. Or send a crowd of friends to crosstrack your track instead of just one or two. Or have the crowd cross your track on a corner. Or have your friends picnic on one of your legs as you run your track. Keep these proofing tracks otherwise simple and fun so you will clarify the issue of staying on the track whatever else happens rather than overwhelming the dog with unusual happenings. See the discussion on page 156 for more ideas.

Remember to intersperse easy motivational tracks every few sessions. The frequency of motivational tracks depends on your dog's temperament. Keep him motivated by controlling the difficulty of your main tracks and by using motivational tracks often.

Discussion:

A TDX test-like track must have the following features:
- Age: 3-5 hours old
- Length: 800-1000 yards
- Corners: 5-7 corners (at least 3 must be 90°, some out in the open)
- Crosstracks: two laid about 90 minutes after the main track
- Obstacles: at least 2 difficult obstacles or compound obstacles.

A sample test map is reproduced below. The dog on this track passed.

Have a trusted experienced tracking friend lay the test-like track. Don't use flags or markers. Make sure the tracklayer makes a good map and can show you the location of the track anywhere the dog gets lost. Have two other people lay the crosstracks and remove the crosstrack flags.

Run the track much like you would run the track in a test. But do set up some simple rule for the track-layer to know when to offer you help. For example, help me when my dog and I get more than 30 yards from the track. In a real test, many judges will give you more than 30 yards, but here you want to avoid mis-training your dog by letting him stray too far from the track. If things start to go badly, immediately switch into training mode and have the tracklayer keep you continuously informed of the direction of the track. Do not allow these mini-tests to become a bad experience for the dog.

Have the tracklayer count the number of different times he had to help you plus the number of times you could see the track and you helped the dog yourself. Have the tracklayer remind you of that number after the track is over. No help means you pass the practice test; help in even one place means you didn't. Whether or not you pass, talk over your handling and the dog's performance with the tracklayer. Get ideas for where you need more work and what things are going well.

If you pass one of these tests, evaluate the track yourself to see if it is really up to test-like standards. If so, count it as permission to think about entering a test. As you go about finding tests to enter and trying to get in, keep up the practice test procedure every few weeks. You want to maintain at least a 33% pass rate on test-like practice tracks. A 50% rate would be even better. Keep learning from the experience, keep working on your strong and weak points, keep motivated, and both you and your dog will continue to improve your likelihood of passing the test you do get into.

Other tracks should be similar to those in phase C. Most of them should be short (500-700 yards) and focused on one or two specific issues. Every once in a while lay a long simple track (1000 yards). All but your motivational tracks should be older than 2 hours.

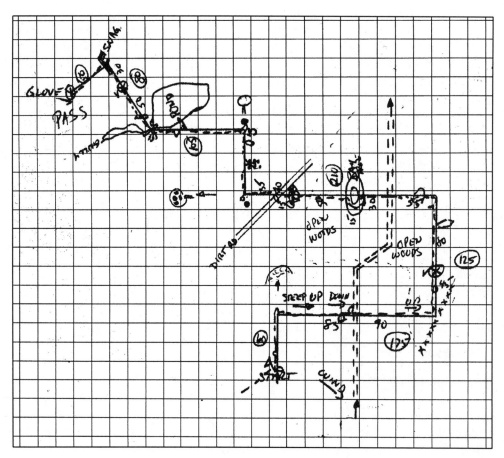

Phase E. Preparing for the Test.

Strategy:

- Familiarize you and your dog with test-like terrain and tracking conditions.
- Teach your dog to ignore and overcome common handler errors.
- Peak your dog's performance for the test.

Discussion

See Phase 8 for a full discussion of test preparation. It is doubly important before a TDX test:
- to expose your dog to the type of terrain that he will face in a test,
- to prepare him to ignore and overcome common handler errors,
- to have him and you in top physical condition,
- to have him highly motivated.

Use the techniques described in Phase 8 adapted to the TDX test.

In particular:
- Find out all you can about the test site. Call the test secretary to find a contact who knows the site. Track at the site or a good substitute well before the test.
- Proof common handling errors with great rewards right after the handler error.
- Peak your handling performance and your dog's tracking performance for the test.
- On your test track, read your dog, trust him, and communicate your confidence in his skill.
- If he gets in trouble, keep yourself oriented in the field, organize his search, get him to circle, back up, trust him and go with him.

A Final Word Or Two

This is fun! You and your dog can do it! Enjoy yourself! Enjoy the process!

Tracking is a wonderful sport. If you have had a great time training, you may want to go on to train for the VST tests. This test is of similar complexity to the TDX but uses many different vegetated and non-vegetated surfaces in an urban or suburban setting. In addition, if you are interested in Search and Rescue, you will find your dog's tracking skill a necessary component of the many additional skills you and he will need to become a certified Search and Rescue dog.

"Unusual" Conditions Often Found at TDX Tests

Expose your dog on otherwise easy tracks to many of the following situations so if it happens to you in a test, you and the dog will be able to handle it. Although a few of these conditions might earn you an alternate track, you want to pass the first track you attempt because the alternate track is often the worst track of the day. In training you will want to mark the track near these unusual conditions.

- Change of cover near the start or a footpath near the start.
- No article at start - tracklayer did not leave it.
- Article at start is blown off the track – toss it 6-10 feet to the side.
- Intermediate article blown off track.
- Intermediate article is a leather glove or a really cool toy.
- Corner at an article, right before, or right after an article.
- Crosstracks near an obstacle, near a change of cover.
- Crosstracks over a corner.
- Crosstracks laid by a pregnant woman, by youngsters, or by someone with a limp.
- Crosstracks laid with short heavy steps.
- Crosstracks laid by a car or truck crossing the track in grass.
- Crosstracks laid by a horse and rider.
- Crosstracks laid by an open vehicle such as a golf cart.
- Group of "bird-watchers" crossing the track.
- Hikers cross the track at about the same time it is laid.
- Hikers standing on the track when it is run.
- Horses gallop over the track or people on horses ride over the track.
- 4-wheel drive vehicles drive over the track.
- Tracklayer is a smoker, heavily perfumed, or vice-versa - whatever the dog is not used to.
- Tracklayer is very nervous or very stressed.
- Flag left along track or flag fallen over near the track.
- Loose dogs on track while it is being laid or while it is being run.
- Barking dogs the other side of a fence from the track.
- Track is near a busy road. For safety, have a chain-link fence between the track and the road.
- Dog is taken out to the track in the back of a strange noisy smelly vehicle.

Bibliography

Alex, Richard, "The molecular logic of scent", *Scientific American*, v. 273, no. 4, pp. 154, Oct. 1995.

Barnard, John F., "On the right track", AKC Gazette, v. 115, no. 3, pp. 54, March 1998.

Brown, Wentworth, *Bring Your Nose Over Here*, ASAP Printing, Albuquerque, NM, 1984.

Button, Lou, *Practical Scent Dog Training*, Alpine Publications, Loveland, CO, 1990.

Chadwick, Derek, Joan Marsh & Jamie Goode, eds., *The Molecular Basis of Smell and Taste Transduction*, Wiley, Chichester, NY, 1993.

Davis, L. Wilson, *Go Find!*, Howell Book House, New York, NY, 1974.

Dold, Catherine, "For rescue dogs nothing's is better than a live find", *Smithsonian*, v. 28, no. 5, pp. 72-82, August 1997.

Ganz, Sandy & Susan Boyd, *Tracking Dog Excellent*, Show-Me Publications, St. Louis, MO, 1992.

Ganz, Sandy & Susan Boyd, *Tracking From the Ground Up*, Show-Me Publications, St. Louis, 1989.

Hunter, Roy, *Fun Nosework for Dogs*, Howln Moon Press, Eliot, ME, 1994

Johnson, Glen R., *Tracking Dog - Theory And Methods*, Arner Publications, Inc., Canastota, NY, 1977. The except on page 114 is used with the kind permission of Arner Publications, Inc.

Kearney, Jack, *Tracking - A Blueprint for Learning How*, Pathways Press, El Cajon, CA 1986.

Koehler, William R., *Training Tracking Dogs*, Howell Book House, New York, 1984.

Krause, Carolyn, *The Puppy Tracking Primer*, Firedog Enterprises, Springfield, MO, 1992.

Persnall, Ed & Christy Bergeon, *Component Training for Variable Surface Tracking*, PawMark Press, Katy, TX, 1998.

Pearsall, Milo D. & Hugo Verbruggen, M.D., *Scent*, Alpine Publications, Loveland, CO, 1982.

Pollard, Hugh B. C., *The Mystery of Scent*, Eyre and Spottiswoode, London, 1937.

Syrotuck, William G., *Scent and the Scenting Dog*, Arner Publications, Westmoreland, NY, 1972.

Theses, A., Steen, J. B., Doving, K. B., "Behavior of dogs during olfactory tracking", *Journal of Experimental Biology*, Vol. 180, 247-251, July 1993.

Tracking Club of Massachusetts, *Tracking : a guide for beginners*, Wakefield, Mass, 1986.